Professional Learning in Early Childhood Settings

Professional Learning
Volume 3

Series editor:

J. John Loughran, *Monash University, Clayton, Australia*

Editorial board:

Renee Clift - *University of Illinois, Urbana-Champaign, USA*

Ruth Kane - *Massey University, New Zealand*

Mieke Lunenberg - *Free University, The Netherlands*

Anthony Clarke - *University of British Columbia, Canada*

Donald Freeman - *School for International Training, Vermont, USA*

MOK, Mo Ching Magdalena - *Hong Kong Institute of Education, Hong Kong*

Max van Manen - *University of Alberta, Canada*

Rationale:

This series purposely sets out to illustrate a range of approaches to Professional Learning and to highlight the importance of teachers and teacher educators taking the lead in reframing and responding to their practice, not just to illuminate the field but to foster genuine educational change.

Audience:

The series will be of interest to teachers, teacher educators and others in fields of professional practice as the context and practice of the pedagogue is the prime focus of such work. Professional Learning is closely aligned to much of the ideas associated with reflective practice, action research, practitioner inquiry and teacher as researcher.

Professional Learning in Early Childhood Settings

Susan Edwards
Monash University, Australia

Joce Nutall
Monash University, Australia

SENSE PUBLISHERS
ROTTERDAM / TAIPEI

A C.I.P. record for this book is available from the Library of Congress.

ISBN 978-90-8790-748-8 (paperback)
ISBN 978-90-8790-749-5 (hardback)
ISBN 978-90-8790-750-1 (ebook)

Published by: Sense Publishers,
P.O. Box 21858, 3001 AW
Rotterdam, The Netherlands
http://www.sensepublishers.com

Printed on acid-free paper

CONTENTS

ELIZABETH WOOD

FOREWORD

Professional learning in early childhood settings

INTRODUCTION

The field of early childhood education is undergoing rapid developments, as evidenced by international recognition of the importance of early childhood education, the implementation of policy frameworks, and substantial funding to improve provision and services in developed and developing countries. At the same time, many questions have been raised about dominant narratives in the field, particularly those that privilege western theories, approaches and worldviews. Susan Edwards and Joce Nuttall have succeeded in bringing together new and established researchers in the field, whose work is focused on the continuing endeavour to reconceptualise early childhood education in relation to social and cultural diversity. They define a clear theoretical rationale for adopting post-developmental perspectives by presenting articulate justifications of why beliefs and practices need to change, and the contrasting ways in which such changes can come about. This sets the scene for critical engagement with the dynamic relationships between theory, policy and practice, and for exploring new methodologies.

Many national and regional governments have moved towards common curriculum frameworks, which are often implemented via 'top-down' models of professional development. This book is, therefore, timely in its conceptualisation and content. The contributors expand notions of professional learning in early childhood education and care from the somewhat limited policy-driven models, to approaches that embrace multi-disciplinary, as well as ethical, political and philosophical perspectives. They demonstrate that some of the most creative innovations are taking place within early childhood education, in terms of challenging dominant western views of children's learning and development, and exploring new theoretical ideas about curriculum, pedagogy, workforce development and professional learning. These innovations are being driven by the willingness of the academic and practitioner communities to engage in collaborative research, and create new understandings through exploring the tensions and dilemmas that arise in the complex contexts of everyday practice. The contributors are also open and honest about the struggles and challenges of change processes, particularly in confronting personal as well as institutional power. It is through the creation of critical learning cultures that professionals can bring about incremental changes that may lead over time to more radical shifts.

In the context of contemporary concerns with diversity, equity and social justice, this book can be seen as a catalyst for critical engagement with taken for granted assumptions, and as a springboard for further enquiry. The clear message that all early childhood professionals need to challenge beliefs and practices in the context of the complex social, cultural, economic and technological changes that are happening in the 21st century.

Professor Elizabeth Wood
University of Exeter I

SUSAN EDWARDS AND JOCE NUTTALL

1. INTRODUCTION

Professional learning in early childhood settings

INTRODUCTION

This book examines the nature and purposes of professional learning in early childhood settings from post-developmental theoretical perspectives. The aims of the book are modest. Debates about professional learning in non-compulsory educational settings are few in comparison to the growing literature related to educators in schools. So, in order to foster similar debates in early childhood education, we have invited each of the contributors to this book to conceptualise professional learning in relation to changing cultural, social, economic, and technological times, and to describe the ways in which they see these changes intersecting with new perspectives about educators, children, and learning in early childhood education. They have responded with fascinating insights into emerging methodologies of professional learning in prior-to-school settings, through a series of case studies drawn from research and practice in Australia, New Zealand, and the United Kingdom.

In this introduction we describe the framework for this book and some propositions about professional learning in early childhood by posing the series of questions to which the chapter authors were invited to respond: What is professional learning? Where does early childhood professional learning occur? What role are post developmental perspectives playing in current approaches to professional learning? And, based on the authors' experience, research, and practice, What are the challenges facing the early childhood field with respect to professional learning? In inviting contributions from authors from the United Kingdom, New Zealand, and Australia, we seek to expand on developing notions of professional learning in early childhood education and care.

WHAT IS PROFESSIONAL LEARNING?

The phrase 'professional learning' is, in itself, relatively new to early childhood education. Indeed, debates about what it means to be a 'professional' in early childhood services are alive and well, as evidenced by Carmen Dalli and Sue Cherrington in Chapter 5 of this volume. Writers about professional learning in educational settings have typically resisted attempts to develop unitary definitions of professional learning (see, for example, the range of positions taken in Clemens, Berry, & Kostagriz, 2007). This stance is a response to the ways in which the

S. Edwards, and J. Nuttall (eds.), Professional Learning in Early Childhood Settings, 1–8.

nature, processes, and purposes of professional learning are highly dependent upon specific social, cultural, economic, historical, and interpersonal contexts.

Many readers will be more familiar with the term 'professional development' as a signifier of continuing workplace learning. Perhaps the shift from 'development' to 'learning' simply reflects official discourses of 'lifelong learning'. Alternatively, it may reflect the increasing acceptance of constructivist notions of 'teachers as co-constructors' of children's learning. Either way, we should not accept such discursive shifts uncritically. What is gained and what is lost in the move from 'development' to 'learning'? A potential loss is that change will become equated with shifts in educators' cognition, without these shifts necessarily being operationalised in practice, or interrogated from ethical or philosophical positions. Without succumbing to reductive notions of mind versus body, or theory versus practice, it is possible to see that a discourse of 'learning' may devalue the rich complexity of educators' working theories, embodied through practice, unless researchers and academics take care to acknowledge and respect the dialectical relationship between practice and theory. On the other hand, what may be gained in resisting discourses of development is an end to the sense that professional development is something that is 'done to' educators, with educators reduced to passive consumers of the latest policy-driven changes in curriculum and pedagogy. These ideas feature heavily in the writings of the various chapter authors. For example, Alma Fleet and Catherine Patterson (Chapter 2) and Mindy Blaise (Chapter 3) each examine processes associated with professional learning that explicitly move away from a model of professional learning based on developmental or career 'stages'. Instead, these authors call for understandings of professional learning that are locally situated and strongly challenge the relevance of 'one-day-one-stop' professional learning experiences for early childhood professionals.

The question of what constitutes professional learning will also depend upon the theoretical perspective(s) of the students, practitioners, researchers, and academics who engage with this book. It is exciting to see the range of entry points adopted by various authors in this book; for example, Joce , Nuttall's use of sociocultural theory (Chapter 7), Jan Georgesons' use of cultural-historical activity theory (Chapter 8), Mindy Blaise's use of post-structural theory (Chapter 3), and Alma Fleet and Catherine Patterson's use of narrativity (Chapter 2). Each of the theoretical perspectives taken in this book is a response to, and outgrowth of, the meta-narrative of 'development' that dominated early childhood services, as well as professional learning, for most of the twentieth century in countries such as New Zealand, Australia, and the United Kingdom. A unifying feature of this response is the importance of understanding professional learning in terms of the professional contexts in which early childhood educators are engaged. The situated nature of learning is valued for contributing to professional understandings that allow professionals to grow their ideas and understandings about children and childhood in ways that honour the challenges and complexities associated with working, and learning, in early childhood settings.

WHY TAKE A POST-DEVELOPMENTAL PERSPECTIVE?

Frameworks for understanding teaching and learning in early childhood settings are undergoing rapid revision. This partly derives from the ways in which technology is driving social and economic change and, in doing so, redrawing the boundaries of childhood (Prout, 2005). Re-thinking childhood demands a re-think of the theories informing early education and how these theories imply new forms of practice. It is now common to read of 'contested childhoods' and 'multiple world views' as arguments against the previously dominant, singular, and universal conception of childhood and child development (Cannella, 2005, p. 18). Many readers of this book will have learned, as student teachers, to plan for play and focus on children's development from a Piagetian perspective. Within this framework, change in children was understood according to a pre-ordained developmental continuum and had little to do with educators' capacity to respond to contemporary society. Now, early childhood care and education is shifting its focus from the developing individual to an awareness of learning across a range of social, economic, gendered, and cultural communities:

It is apparent that in contemporary times the skills of early childhood educators are broadening and are being reconceptualised from practitioners who do *what is said to be right*, to practitioners who ask, *In what ways can we create effective learning environments?* The new aspects of practitioners' discourse are the result of living in more complex and uncertain times which have lead to the emergence of multifaceted questions and issues regarding the ethical considerations of practice, the cultural ramifications of practice and the consideration of equity in education. Maintaining currency and relevance in the early childhood sector requires a continual engagement with critical issues, as well as finding new ways to adapt to changing educational circumstances. (Yelland, & Kilderry, 2005, p. 7, italics in original)

Post-developmental perspectives in early childhood education are also shaping the discourse surrounding the creation of learning environments. This is because post-developmentalists emphasise ethical issues, cultural contexts, and the struggle for equity in the provision of learning experiences. Post-developmental theoretical perspectives, including cultural historical theory, post-structuralism, feminism, and post-modernism, have been used to question *whose* development, *whose* learning, *whose* beliefs, and *whose* values are supported and enacted in early learning settings (Ball & Pence, 2000; Brooker, 2005; MacNaughton, 1997; 2005; Ritchie, 2002). Post-developmental views, particularly those which emphasise the socially situated nature of learning, are also increasingly found in the formalized curriculum documents developed in many OECD countries (for example, the Czech Republic, Finland, France, Hungary, Italy, Korea, Mexico, New Zealand, Norway, Portugal, Sweden and the United Kingdom [Organisation for Economic Co-operation and Development, 2006, pp. 265 – 425]). Early childhood educators' work has become increasingly focussed on the child-in-context as the starting point of planning for learning, rather than starting from developmental norms and planning for individual developmental needs. This approach moves educators beyond technical-rationalism toward critical engagement with questions of substance relevant to childhood and to education:

> Critical thinking enables us to speak of questions and possibilities rather than givens and necessities. It shows us there are choices to be made between possibilities, that the usual way of proceeding is not self-evident, that there is no one 'best practice' or standard of quality' to be found (since such concepts are always value-laden and relative), that there may be more than one possible answer to any question. Moreover, these choices are not just between different methods or solutions, seeking an answer to the zeitgeist question of 'what works?' The choices are more fundamental, and require us first to formulate questions: 'what do we want for our children?', 'what is a good childhood', 'what is the place of children in society?', 'who do we think children are?', 'what are the purposes of institutions/services/spaces for children?', 'what is education for?', 'what do we mean by care?' – and so on. The answers to these questions – even 'what works?' cannot be reduced to the technical and managerial. They require choices to be made that are ethical and political in nature, and a recognition and acceptance of the responsibility that goes with making such choices (Moss & Petrie, 2002, p. 11).

So far, we have summarised recent trends that extend beyond developmental theory to thinking about young children's learning in more complex and situated ways. What, then, might this mean for the learning of their educators? As shifts occur in the theoretical perspectives brought to bear on children's learning, shifts must also occur in thinking about how *adults* learn in early childhood settings.

WHAT DO WE KNOW ABOUT PROFESSIONAL LEARNING IN EARLY CHILDHOOD SETTINGS?

We argued at the beginning of this chapter that professional learning is relatively under-explored in early childhood settings. One thing we do know, however, is that moving beyond developmentalism and technical-rational models of practice, towards more complex ways of thinking about teaching young children, is rarely easy. Susan Edwards (in Chapter 6) examines early childhood educators' conceptions of cultural-historical theory as an informant to their practice, and highlights how such movement challenges educators' certainty and expertise, "leaving in its wake questions regarding who the educator is and what the children are learning from the program" (Edwards, 2006, p. 250). Mindy Blaise's description of the local politicalisation of a group of educators, described in Chapter 3, and Judy Walker's account of a developing group of hospital play specialists (Chapter 4) likewise demonstrate how such considerations go to the heart of educators' identities and subjectivities. These identities are just as vulnerable to normalising discourses of 'care' and 'education', as they are to particular constructions of children and childhood. For example, Sumsion's (2004) exploration of early childhood educators' resilience in the face of stressful workplace circumstances reminds us that there are also prevalent discourses about early childhood educators that function to maintain existing oppressive structures:

> Dominant cultural scripts and discourses position early childhood teachers as preternaturally stoic, compliant, self-sacrificing and motivated primarily by the intrinsic rewards of working with young children (Duncan, 1996; Lyons, 1996). As such, they can lead to complacency amongst employers, policy makers, teacher educators and influential others, and complicity in not doing more to challenge and contest adverse structural factors that have led to high attrition rates (Sumison, 2004, p. 288).

Whilst new ways of thinking about professional learning have the potential to support consciousness raising and new (and potentially transgressive) practices, the structural factors identified by Sumison are extraordinarily persistent. In Chapter 7, for example, Joce Nuttall describes the staffing arrangements of community-based kindergartens in Victoria, Australia, which have remained unchanged since the late 1800s. In an era of rapid professionalisation and intensification of kindergarten teaching, the structure of kindergarten programs serves to severely curtail educators' access to professional learning and, in doing so, reduces the likelihood that they will understand and challenge the oppressive conditions under which they work.

Mitchell and Cubey's (2003) synthesis of research into professional learning in early childhood settings identifies some of the factors that have the potential to challenge structural limitations, including: the provision of adequate time for collaboration between educators; the provision of skilled external facilitation; and positive attitudes toward ongoing learning amongst the educators' themselves. Each of these factors is dependant, however, upon political will (i.e. funding) in order to be realised. These factors are realised in the descriptions of professional learning presented by Alma Fleet and Catherine Patterson (in Chapter 2) and Judy Walker (Chapter 4). Here, the authors contrast the success and otherwise, of narrative driven professional learning in hospital, prior to school, and primary school settings. These chapters highlight the importance of collaborative endeavour between professionals and the facilitators of professional learning when seeking to facilitate adult learning. Walker's chapter bears testimony to the determination of play specialists to pursue ongoing professional learning, explore new theoretical standpoints, and risk alternative practices, even in the face of structures that serve to limit the agency of educators, children and families. Like other chapters in this book, these authors challenge early childhood researchers, academics, and professional educators to go beyond the time-honoured, one-day, one-stop approach to 'professional development' and to view early childhood professionals as active inquirers into their own professional learning (Moss, 2006; Goodfellow & Hedges, 2007).

Research evidence suggesting a causal link between educators' ongoing learning, increased service quality, and improved later educational outcomes for children (Aitken & Kennedy, 2007; Gammage, 2006), has been used in some countries (notably New Zealand and the United Kingdom, and more recently

Australia), to support early childhood education and care through increased funding and targeted policy measures. This was illustrated by New Zealand's then Minister of Education, the Rt. Hon. Trevor Mallard, who exemplified the politically persuasive nature of the connection between ongoing professional learning and quality educational outcomes for young children when he launched the early childhood assessment resource, *Kei Tua o te Pae* (Ministry of Education, 2004), pledging NZ$12million to support professional learning programs to roll out the resource:

> The exemplars consist of a series of books that help teachers to understand and strengthen children's learning and how children, parents and whānau [extended family] can contribute to this assessment and ongoing learning... More than $12 million is being spent to develop this resource and provide professional development on assessment for early childhood teachers. I am pleased to be part of a government that recognises the importance of early learning experiences and values early childhood education. (Hon Trevor Mallard, Minister of Education, press release, 17 January 2005)

Research that explores the link between educators' professional learning and children's learning has been seized upon by UK politicians to justify more comprehensive programs of professional support. Despite this, most early childhood educators in the UK (and elsewhere), still do not have access to adequate, long-term, resources to support their professional learning. Jan Georgeson (Chapter 8) examines recent policy initiatives in England intended to ensure degree qualified staff in all early childhood services by 2012. Drawing on activity theory, Georgeson offers a cautionary tale to readers in New Zealand and Australia as she considers the implications of policy-driven professional learning as a means to realise increased learning outcomes for children. Georgeson suggests that care is needed to ensure a balance between theoretical and contextually relevant knowledge when developing learning programs for young children.

HOW MIGHT WE INVESTIGATE PROFESSIONAL LEARNING IN EARLY CHILDHOOD SETTINGS?

The central claim of this book is that the efforts of researchers and practitioners to participate in and make sense of professional learning in early childhood settings can be driven by post-developmental theories in ways that challenge traditional assumptions about both children's and adult's learning. We believe that this perspective is essential to maintaining the vigour and energy that is presently driving early childhood education research, pedagogy, policy development, and professional learning towards new ways of teaching and learning. These perspectives reduce the risk of contemporary claims about educators and children 'learning together' becoming yet another meta-narrative of early childhood education. Rather, post-developmental perspectives on professional learning allow the highly complex, problematic, and often troubling work of early childhood educators to be examined. Inevitably, such examinations lead to broader questions around policy as well as practice, suggesting the need for initiatives that not only support the professionalisation of the field, but also provide meaningful links between curriculum implementation and professional learning.

As the chapters in this volume attest, post-developmental perspectives challenge old approaches to professional development, and describe new ways of creating contextually relevant and culturally significant learning for early childhood professionals. This movement is mirrored by changes in the field of early childhood curriculum and pedagogy, which likewise emphasize the creation of socially situated and culturally engaging learning experiences for young children. Recognizing these twin developments holds out the promise of a new future in early childhood professional learning research, as the nexus between post-developmental perspectives and their role in challenging both children's and adult's learning is examined. The implications of this research agenda for professional learning, and its relationship to policy and practice, is examined in the concluding chapter of this book.

REFERENCES

Aitken, H., & Kennedy, A. (2007). Critical issues for the early childhood profession. In L. Keesing-Styles & H. Hedges (Eds.), *Theorising early childhood practice: Emerging dialogues* (pp. 165–187). Castle Hill, New South Wales: Pademelon Press.

Ball, J., & Pence, A. (2000). A postmodernist approach to culturally grounded training in early childhood care and development. *Australian Journal of Early Childhood, 25*(1), 21–25.

Brooker, L. (2005). Learning to be a child: Cultural diversity and early years ideology. In N. Yelland (Ed.), *Critical issues in early childhood education* (pp. 115–130). Berkshire, England: Open University Press.

Cannella, G. (2005). Reconceptualising the filed (of early care and education): If 'western' child development is a problem, then what do we do? In N. Yelland (Ed.), *Critical issues in early childhood education* (pp. 17–40). Berkshire, England: Open University Press.

Clemens, A., Berry A., &.Kostagriz, A. (Eds.). (2006). *Changing perspectives on professional learning professionalism, identities and practice*. Rotterdam, The Netherlands: Sense Publishers.

Edwards, S. (2006). 'Stop thinking of culture as geography': Early childhood educators' conceptions of sociocultural theory as an informant to curriculum. *Contemporary Issues in Early Childhood, 7*(3), 238–252.

Gammage, P. (2006). Early childhood education and care: Politics, policies and possibilities. *Early Years. International Journal of Research and Development, 26*(3), 235–248.

Goodfellow, J., & Hedges, H. (2007). Practitioner research 'centre stage': Contexts, contributions and challenges. In L. Keesing-Styles & H. Hedges (Eds.), *Theorising early childhood practice: Emerging dialogues* (pp. 187–207). Castle Hill, New South Wales: Pademelon Press.

MacNaughton, G. (1997). Feminist praxis and the gaze in the early childhood curriculum. *Gender and Education, 9*(3), 317–326.

Ministry of Education. (2004). *Kei tua o te pae. Assessment for learning: Early childhood exemplars*. Wellington, New Zealand: Learning Media.

Mitchell, L., & Cubey, P. (2003). *Characteristics of professional development linked to enhanced pedagogy and children's learning in early childhood settings: Best evidence synthesis*. Wellington, New Zealand: Ministry of Education.

Moss, P. (2006). Structures, understandings and discourses: Possibilities for re-envisioning the early childhood worker. *Contemporary Issues in Early Childhood, 7*(1), 30–41.

Moss, P., & Petrie, P. (2002). *From children's services to children's spaces: Public policy, children and childhood.* London: Routledge Falmer.

Prout, A. (2005). *The future of childhood.* London: Routledge Falmer.

Organisation for Economic Cooperation and Development. (2006). *Starting strong II: Early childhood education and care.* Paris: OECD Publishing.

Rhedding-Jones, J. (2005). Decentering Anglo-American curricular power in early childhood education: Learning, culture and 'child development' in higher education coursework. *Journal of Curriculum Theorizing, 21*(3), 133–153.

Ritchie, J. (2002). Bicultural development: Innovation in implementation of Te Whariki. *Australian Journal of Early Childhood, 28*(2), 32–37.

Sumison, J. (2004). Early childhood teachers' construction of their resilience and thriving: A continuing investigation. *International Journal of Early Years Education, 12*(3), 275–290.

Yelland, N., & Kilderry, A. (2005). Against the tide: New ways of in early childhood education. In N. Yelland (Ed.), *Critical issues in early childhood education* (pp. 1–15). Berkshire, England: Open University Press.

Susan Edwards
Centre for Childhood Studies
Faculty of Education
Monash University
Joce Nuttall
Centre for Childhood Studies
Faculty of Education
Monash University

ALMA FLEET AND CATHERINE PATTERSON

2. A TIMESCAPE

Personal Narratives - Professional Spaces

INTRODUCTION

Our lives are ceaselessly intertwined with narrative, with the stories that we tell and hear told, with the stories that we dream or imagine or would like to tell. All these stories are reworked in that story of our own lives which we narrate to ourselves in an episodic, sometimes semiconscious, virtually uninterrupted monologue. We live immersed in narrative, recounting and reassessing the meanings of our past actions, anticipating the outcomes of our future projects, situating ourselves at the intersection of several stories not yet completed (Polkinghorne, 1988, p. 160).

This chapter examines the ways in which narrative accounts of educators' thinking can be used both conceptually and methodologically to understand and provoke adult learning in early childhood settings. Drawing on research conducted by the authors, the chapter emphasises the growing irrelevance of traditional single session professional development. Increasingly, educational contexts demand pedagogical thoughtfulness and analytical reflection in order to meet the challenges of multiple communities living in complex spaces. The professional growth of educators has thus become one "of the proliferation of arenas in which the often unexpectedly aggressive if subtle action of narrative is now found to be at work" (Nash, 1990, p. xii).

CHALLENGING ORTHODOXIES AND NOMENCLATURE

The construct of professional development has become problematic. One of the challenges lies in a conceptualisation which presumes that workers will move from being less professional to more professional as part of a developmental continuum. VanderVen, for example, wrote from this perspective in 1988, presenting an analysis of differentiated roles and quantities of supervision required at different stages of development. In contrast we noted in 2001 that:

The application of developmental stage theory to peoples' lives ignores the complexity of workplace circumstances and the role of interaction in supporting the social construction of staff professional knowledge The importance of a philosophy of staff ownership of ideas rather than

S. Edwards, and J. Nuttall (eds.), Professional Learning in Early Childhood Settings, 9–25.

transmission of knowledge is a critical component in conceptions of growth possibilities as multi-layered and fluid (Fleet & Patterson, 2001, p. 14).

What follows are some multi-faceted stories of practice; they are predominantly our story, a narrative that engages with the constructs embedded in professional growth. The stories of our history reflect changes in the conceptualisations of professional learning as well as a sequence of experiences with educators drawing on notions of 'provocation' and 'narrative'.

> In this narrative view of teachers' knowledge, we mean more than teachers telling stories of specific children and events. We mean that their way of being in the classroom is storied: As teachers they are characters in their own stories of teaching, which they author (Connelly & Clandinin, 1995, p. 12).

This then is our stage for presenting narratives of professional growth – two colleagues using storytelling as a tool to reflect on their practices as teacher educators and to generate richer narratives for professional learning. These personal perspectives on professional narratives are offered to invite a wider conversation. Narratives are recognised as having a 'rich role' in social life (Czarniawska, 2004, p. 1) and thus provide a productive device for generating understandings relating to those who live and work in social settings. This has been shown clearly in the writings of authors such as Chase (1995), when investigating empowerment through the professional stories of senior women in school administration, and Fishman and McCarthy (2000), whose records of their own conversations provided a personal history of their collaborations.

Yelland (2005) reminds us that early childhood educators are working and thinking in a complex climate that foregrounds reconceptualisation of earlier taken-for-granted pedagogies, practices and concomitant discourses. From that perspective, the following timescape provides a historical frame for an evolution of ideas and a context for confronting traditional discourses of 'professional development'.

CONSTRUCTING A NARRATIVE

This story of our shared fascination with research into professional learning begins over a decade ago. At that time, there was growing interest among teacher educators in the use of teacher stories (Clandinin, Davies, Hogan & Kennard, 1993; Connelly & Clandinin, 1998), and classroom cases (Shulman, 1991) in professional development. These narrative approaches to teacher education were not new. Indeed, in his 1990 paper Doyle pointed out that "in the mid-nineteenth century, Sheldon (1864) used cases to illustrate how the project method worked in classrooms" (p. 8).

The resurgence of interest in narrative approaches in the 1990s can be related to several factors. In the foreword to McAninch (1993), Floden suggests that revitalised interest in narrative approaches appeared to grow from a recognition that as "teaching and learning are complex processes, investigators have shifted from seeking simple laws of learning to providing thick descriptions of educational episodes" (p. ix). Second, there was an acknowledgement that narrative approaches could make a valuable contribution to the knowledge base of teaching practice leading to the acceptance of teacher voice and empowerment. A third factor contributing to this renewed interest related to the use of case methods to provide "an opportunity to enhance reflective thinking" for professionals (Richert, 1991, p. 135). Cycles of reflective thought were seen as contributing depth to professional decision-making.

As we were immersing ourselves in this literature in the early 1990s, a national project emerged enabling us to explore the use of case materials to illustrate an early childhood perspective on the quality of teaching and learning (Fleet, Duffie & Patterson, 1993). We drew ideas from a number of publications related to teacher learning through case methods (e.g. Bullough, 1993; Christensen & Hansen, 1987; Doyle, 1990; McAninch, 1993; Merseth, 1991; Richert, 1991; Shulman 1991, 1992; Wassermann, 1993). We visited classrooms and observed teachers at work to capture significant moments to highlight professional practice in the first years of school (Fleet, Duffie & Patterson, 1995).

Reflecting on those vignettes now, we can see that the teachers gained very little professional learning from their involvement in the project. The observations were taken away by the researchers who crafted the material into case materials to provide examples for the project. Unfortunately, teachers were not involved in the writing of the vignettes, nor were they invited to reflect on their experiences. At the time the relevant literature suggested that this was an appropriate approach to creating case materials for the purpose of teacher development.

While our experience with this national project highlighted both the advantages and disadvantages of working with de-contextualised vignettes, we became aware of the richness we were able to bring to our own teaching through the use of scenarios. Student teachers were able to explore possible responses to these examples of contextually-based real-life situations, which added depth and meaning to lectures and tutorials.

TEACHERS' STORIES FOR PROFESSIONAL LEARNING

Building on this interest, twelve months later we received a Macquarie University Teaching Grant to develop a series of cases to support the learning of pre-service teacher education students. Rather than gather information through classroom observations, we decided to invite experienced teachers to work with us and write their own stories. The shift in focus from 'cases' to 'stories' reflected our increased appreciation that stories were able to present the voices of teachers and that case methodology suggested a clinical lens different from our frame of reference. It also reflected a shift in the scholarly literature (see, for example, Fludernik, 1996) in which narrativity was being more broadly interpreted than in the past, moving beyond a temporally bound series of events in literary texts to an experiential, consciousness-oriented frame of reference for lived experiences.

We facilitated the writing process through a series of workshops which encouraged teachers to reflect on critical incidents in their teaching careers

(Patterson & Fleet, 1998). This writing and revising process was designed to expand their understanding of their practice and philosophies, through a focus on the writing process itself and a spiral revisiting of experiences. The resultant stories were a powerful source of learning, both for the writer and the reader. The stories were "true accounts of events experienced by early childhood professionals ... the joys, the pleasures, the dilemmas and the heartaches of working with young children" (Patterson, Fleet & Duffie, 1995, p. v). The inclusion of teacher voices mirrored an increasing interest in educational literature in exploring the place of storying as an approach to professional learning (e.g., Beattie, 1995; Carter, 1993; Jalongo, 1992).

In an argument supporting the use of teachers' stories for professional growth, Jalongo (1992) suggests that "by sharing stories about their classroom experiences, teachers not only gain insight into their own practice, but they also contribute to the storehouse of knowledge about teaching (p. 68)." Jalongo argues that a number of professions used stories as tools for professional contexts. For example, "in medicine, stories are case histories; in law, stories set legal precedents; in business, real and hypothetical stories become scenarios." This strong support for storying was related to a growing understanding of the complexities of teaching and the centrality of teachers' 'personal practical knowledge' (Connelly & Clandinin, 1994, 1998).

Linked to this interest in stories and cases, educational research paid increasing attention to narratives through the use of life histories and teacher biography. Scholars such as Butt, Raymond, McCue and Yamagishi (1992), and Cole and Knowles (1995), explored the relationship between teachers' personal and professional knowledge through these approaches to life cycle research. While we acknowledged the potential contribution of such approaches, and they informed our thinking, our interest began to shift to the realities of everyday life specifically for early childhood educators.

We started to work with a group of practitioners in centres by facilitating a series of workshops designed to capture evolving perspectives on curriculum decision-making in preschools and childcare centres. These workplace-based sessions invited educators to reconsider their ways of working in order to incorporate contemporary early childhood principles (Fleet & Patterson, 1998). This led to research aimed at understanding the complexities of local issues experienced by people who engaged with the provocations we offered during these workshops. Each series of workshops included a request to participants to invite us to three regularly scheduled centre planning meetings. This stage of the research continued over eighteen months. We made repeated visits to fifteen centres to attend planning meetings. The educators were not observed by us as 'other', but included us in ongoing discussions. This collaboration provided opportunities for professional development for both service-based early childhood educators and ourselves through philosophical discussions and practical decision-making about planning and programming for children (Fleet & Patterson, 2002; Patterson & Fleet, 2003). The retelling of daily events became the provocation for reflection, the motivation to engage in reconsideration of taken-for-granted practices. The act of storying practice generated learning for the tellers of the stories.

In reflecting on the implications for professional growth from these experiences, we suggested that there was a need to:

> ...reconceptualise responsive professional development ... to recognise the contexts in which people work, as well as the individuality of each learner. The provision of professional development opportunities that support people must reflect diversity of circumstances as well as building a sense of community (Patterson & Fleet, 2001, p. 69).

Those concerned with professional development were encouraged to consider "collaborative and situation-specific" approaches (ibid).

NEGOTIATING THE CULTURES OF SCHOOLS

Evolving alongside these educational conversations in prior-to-school settings were initiatives in which we were working with colleagues interested in educational change across several schooling sectors. Rather than the collaborative investigations of practice described above, these forays into professional development were prompted by enthusiastic Principals who brought us in as outsiders to provoke newer educational thinking (see, for example, Patterson & Fleet, 1999). In contrast with the previous scenarios, we were not invited into classrooms initially by the people who worked in them nor had there been a perceived need by those teachers for our presence.

Neither invitations to write, nor provocations to re-consider practices, nor seductive examples of success elsewhere, made inroads to the natural reticence of school staff who had their own professional agendas. We were unable to generate enthusiasm for school-wide engagement with the learning possibilities we offered. The greatest connections that were made related to the partnerships with particular teachers (five people in the first years of school who were involved for varying periods from a term to a year across a four year period). In each of these circumstances, one of us spent time in a classroom by invitation, seeing the life of the classroom, getting to know some of the children and the contexts in which teachers' dilemmas were unfolding, then discussing possible interpretations and implications with these teachers. Each individual valued these connections, possibly because of the immediate relevance of the workplace narratives that they generated. While the benefit to specific individuals was palpable, the sequential nature of these partnerships may have meant that there was never a critical mass of teachers interested in reconsidering their practices to affect the culture of the school, or helping to shape a more inclusive learning community.

In the context of this chapter, the focus for the Principals could be seen as educational change within the discourse of school improvement, rather than as the professional right of individuals to revisit their practice for improved outcomes within a learning community. From another perspective, the socio-political context could be seen as inimical to reflective professional learning. For example, teachers at one public school were constantly disrupted by a transient student population leading to falling school enrolments, with resultant staff changes, and an inopportune retirement which resulted in the sequential arrival of four school Principals over a five year period. Despite working with the school over an extended period, a collaborative relationship did not evolve in which narrative-related inquiry might flourish. Instead, the teachers remained professionally committed to other school agendas, devoting long hours to more traditional in-service courses and employer-sponsored programs. In an otherwise fluid work environment, these opportunities may have seemed more supportive to teachers than our apparently open-ended provocations. An early successful phase of the project at one school was also interrupted by state-wide industrial action which blocked the after-school meetings in which interested teachers had been sharing stories and examples of practice as provocations for joint discussion. The seeds of collaborative inquiry had been sown, but the structural and cultural conditions were not present to sustain growth.

ENGAGING IN PRACTITIONER INQUIRY

This interest in collaborative inquiry has become the focus of our present attempts to facilitate professional learning in schools and early childhood centres. Our work now concentrates on practitioner inquiry that recognises the professional educator as a powerful, competent learner. Goodfellow and Hedges (2007) have stated that practitioner inquiry is "seen to be potentially transformative in its capacity to lead to better understandings and improved practices" (p. 188).

Our philosophical shift towards practitioner inquiry as a focus for change has been influenced by provocations from educators in the preschools of Reggio Emilia in Italy. Their challenge to re-consider our image of the child to see a learner who is "strong, powerful and rich in potential" (Rinaldi, 2006, p. 123) has caused us to re-consider our own image of the adult as a co-researcher with children. For example, the New South Wales Curriculum Framework (NSW Department of Community Services, 2002) refers to a child who is seen "as capable and resourceful". This child is conceptualised as one with "strength, power, rights, competence, complexity and possibility" (p. 21). Building on this conceptualisation enables us to recast the image of the adults who work with children in a similar light. This 'capable and resourceful' adult learner inspires practitioner inquiry projects that recognize principles of adult learning. These include the importance of:

– building on learner strengths;
– engaging in relevant situationally-based content;
– enabling peer support;
– avoiding confrontation, but challenging counter-productive behaviours; and,
– encouraging participation through a range of supportive strategies.

Maintaining this focus on adults as learners provides a philosophical framework for conceptualising professional growth. Systematic engagement in inquiry over time is a powerful model for professional learning. Practitioner inquiry empowers participants through the gaining of both research skills and knowledge formation in a local context. It is powerful in that over time, a cycle of investigation supported by facilitators can awaken participants with diverse backgrounds to the quality issues present in professional practice, and then to develop skills in addressing those concerns.

During practitioner inquiry projects, we work with people to support their research into elements of practice. Small groups identify a dilemma of practice and create a question to be answered; they gather data about the issue, analyse it and make decisions about pedagogical changes. This type of practitioner inquiry has emerged from the tradition of action research (e.g., Mills, 2000), the acknowledgement of teachers as learners (Groundwater-Smith, Ewing & Le Cornu, 2007), and the valuing of the practitioner's voice in educational improvement (e.g. Fleer & Kennedy, 2006; Hargreaves & Fullan, 1998). We have found this kind of professional opportunity reveals the power of emotional engagement in investigating elements that are of inherent interest to practitioners. Collecting and analysing data about ordinary events and interactions (Manning-Morton, 2006) offers the possibility of building on professional stories for sustained professional growth.

In both schools and prior-to-school centres, we establish 'buddy groups' of practitioners who work together in a continuous spiral of input, action, and reflection. This development of a 'buddy group' learning community (Wenger, 1999) leads to active engagement in issues of immediate concern. There are also benefits for educators in supporting each other rather than relying on solutions presented by 'outside experts'. Our role as facilitators creates a situation where the 'content' we are delivering is philosophically framed to connect with whatever the participants are engaged in. This conceptualisation of professional empowerment through spirals of engagement at multiple levels may include regular gatherings of staff from a number of schools/centres, meetings with all staff in a centre or school, departmental staff teams or room meetings, and small buddy groups. These opportunities for professional exchange support individual agency within sustainable organisational change. The processes depend on locally relevant data collection and analysis, enabling all participants to grow as researchers of their own practice by working in collaborative teams.

This approach contrasts strongly with the impact of traditional approaches to professional learning as noted in the following teacher's reflection:

Many tough situations present themselves within the context of my classroom, situations that tire me. They are not, however, the situations which morally wear me down. The situations that tear at the heart of my practice are the ones in which I am stripped of voice and agency. They are the situations in which someone else's knowledge is delivered to me through the conduit in one place in my professional knowledge landscape and I am expected to enact it as if it were my own in my classroom, another place on my landscape. Living in these two places creates the ongoing, uneasy tensions I have difficulty naming in my practice. It creates the dilemmas that gnaw at my soul (Craig, 1995, p. 24).

The power of this voice reinforces the transformative engagement that narrative inquiry offers, providing opportunities for deep learning beyond those associated with pragmatic, skill-based transmission models of 'professional development'.

The timescape we have described so far has recurrent philosophical and pragmatic threads. Our tale started with small cases, vignettes created through observation and refined through discussion, seeking authenticity for institutional learning contexts, but minimising value for individual story-tellers. We then described a move to critical incidents as provocations. These events were situated in teacher writing workshops which included the elements of group sharing and cycles of analytic reflection. Subsequently, there were explorations of work-based planning decisions, framed as round-table stories of practice over time. Being in situ with colleagues in a shared workspace provided energy and contextualised relevance. Meanwhile, initiatives unfolded in the first years of school, in classrooms where partnerships were fostered and the action-research role of critical friend was nurtured. Finally the journey has taken us to the collaborative landscape of practitioner inquiry. Storying in these contexts evolves in local learning communities, with colleagues researching professional experience and decision-making as part of an ethic of professionalism and personal commitment.

RETHINKING EXPERIENCE

The historical narrative in this chapter has moved us beyond the concept of developing anyone from where they are to where they need to go, which is a linear, hierarchical, and rather patronizing conceptualisation (Fleet & Patterson, 2001). Instead, the narrative has sought the spaces where the voices of educators are present, through the telling and analysing of their own experiences.

Czarniawska (2004) reminds us that, "Narration is a common mode of communication. People tell stories to entertain, to teach and to learn, to ask for an interpretation and to give one" (p. 10). This interactive element is critical and is part of a paradigm change that has radiated through the social sciences.

> The behaviourism that has dominated psychology until recently has given way to an exploration of cognitive processes and purposive action. Philosophers of history have shown that narration is not just an impressionistic substitute for reliable statistics but a method of understanding the past that has its own rationale (Martin, 1986, p. 7).

Taking this shift to the early childhood arena, MacNaughton (2005) has noted, "The most effective professional learning is collaborative, action-focused, dialogical and critically reflective" (p. 198). This thinking also reflects Jones and Nimmo's admonition that:

> In a changing and diverse world, traditional models of a sole source of knowledge and power cannot be effective in sustaining a viable society...teachers need to engage in continuous dialogue with each other and with students. (1999, p. 6)

This argument is similar to approaches to professional learning described by Albrecht and Engel (2007).

The sharing through relationships that accompanies these collegial ponderings reflects an expectation that the understandings garnered from patterns of experience will shape subsequent actions. Through talking, thinking, listening, pausing, imagining possibilities, and reflecting on what is seen, individuals access the data of their own experience and contribute to knowledge generation. Given supportive structural contexts, caring, thoughtful and knowledgeable collaborators can use stories of experience as the yeast of professional learning.

BEYOND TRANSMISSION EVENTS

These conceptualisations blur the boundaries between those on the inside and those on the outside of daily professional practice. Foregrounding narrative can enable the growing to be in a shared space, expanding possibilities both for those working most closely with children and those working to support them. In this context, Bruner (2002) has highlighted for us the power of 'narrative medicine', in which, for example, a "narrative of possible recovery" is being seen as a key component of the medical practitioner's toolkit, where a "shared narrative" is more powerful than "reason alone" (p. 107) in seeking a return to health. In a related study in the Netherlands, Abma (1999) reported on the use of narratives in the collaborative development of meaningful activity to support the re-entrance into society of hospitalised mental patients. Similarly, in trying to understand the expanding circle of ideas and insights about everyday practice in education, the traditional hierarchies associated with professional development are being challenged. Developers become learners and participants are co-constructors of knowledge (see also Nuttall, this volume).

In discussing the problematic nature of transmission-oriented 'professional development programs', Connelly and Clandinin (1995) critiqued the nature and amount of information fed through a "conduit" to teachers in the form of "a rhetoric of conclusions" (p.9). Such approaches deny agency as well as under-representing the importance of practitioners thinking through their own dilemmas and contextualised decision-making as part of their professional learning. Connelly and Clandinin (1995) explain "...we do think that the possibilities for reflective awakenings and transformations are limited when one is alone. Teachers need others in order to engage in conversations where stories can be told, reflected back, heard in different ways, retold, and relived in new ways" (p. 13).

A benefit of privileging this worldview is that it has unbounded potential for being inclusive. Recognising agency and valuing the voices of professionals working with and for children enables the support and inclusion of practitioners of a range of ages, cultural heritage, experience, opportunity and power. It does not presume to predetermine what individuals with particular characteristics (e.g., educational qualifications or ascribed positions) might need, nor does it deify those in positions to support others. This orientation resonates with many elements of practitioner inquiry and the processes inherent in it. Note the following thumbnail sketch of context, philosophy and process within a continuous learning conceptualisation:

> The accountability movement sent educators searching for 'hard data' by which to assess their efforts. What teachers observed came to be considered 'soft data'. Yet we believe the 'hardest', most valuable data available may be the information collected by an *enlightened* teaching team that systematically gathers results over time in the real-life, day-to-day interactions and problem solving of the classroom. To encourage continuous learning for students and staff, teachers must be allowed to design strategies for collecting data. Then they must be allowed to use that assessment data to guide their informed, reflective practice (Costa & Kallick, 2000, p. 27).

This focus on professional learning rather than 'development' is unfolding in parallel with critiques of what MacNaughton (2005) refers to as the 'Training Calendar model' which gives primacy to single session 'fix-it' offerings. In developing her argument, MacNaughton notes that, "It is possible to build Critically Knowing Early Childhood Communities if we are prepared to rethink the knowledge/power relations of existing approaches to professional learning and change that dominate much of the early childhood field" (p. 196). To meet this challenge, she recommends that we recast our models of delivery, targets of 'development' and the content of professional development programs. It is within this context that the seeking and creating of professional narratives within communities of learners becomes germane.

NARRATIVE AND STORYING PRACTICE

In considering storying events as the kernel of cohesion for adult learning opportunities, the essence of narrative is foregrounded. Fostering writing as part of professional learning incorporates the valuing of agency (space for individuals to make decisions about matters concerning them), and phenomenology (study of the every-day as meaningful), as well as narrative, which is seen as both a tool and an empowering process. Polkinghorne (1988) notes that "Narrative displays the significance that events have for one another" (p. 13) and defines narrative as:

> A scheme by means of which human beings give meaning to their experience of temporarily and personal actions. Narrative meaning functions to give form to the understanding of a purpose to life and to join everyday actions and events into episodic units. It provides a framework for understanding the past events of one's life and for planning future actions. It is the primary scheme by means of which human existence is rendered meaningful (ibid, p. 11).

The notion of narrative which is used in this chapter is presented in a variety of forms, none of which reflect the textual analysis or careful attention to extended accounts by individuals which is usually associated with this term. Rather, the narrativity in this account is associated with the importance of story itself as reflective of a philosophical position, as an element of phenomenology, the valuing of lived experience as a foundation for personal professional growth.

As White wrote in 1980:

> So natural is the impulse to narrate, so inevitable is the form of narrative for any report of the way things really happened, that narrative could appear problematical only in a culture in which it was absent – absent or, as in some domains of contemporary Western intellectual and artistic culture, programmatically refused (p. 5).

He then went on to say:

> This suggests that far from being one code among many that a culture may utilize for endowing experience with meaning, narrative is a metacode, a human universal on the basis of which transcultural messages about the nature of a shared reality can be transmitted (p. 6).

This conception of narrative resonates with Himley's (2000) exploration of phenomenology. This 'branch of philosophy' is described as originating at the turn of the century with the work of:

> Edmund Husserl, who understood human consciousness as active, not passive, in making meaning. He argued that we do not just receive the world, but engage with it, and in that active encounter produce what it means. In extending the phenomenological project, Merleau-Ponty described human existence as it is lived at that point of encounter, at the lived point of world and consciousness, where there exists a dynamic relationship of the person and the world. What phenomenology offers then is a particular take on what knowledge is or can be…thus knowledge is understood as always unfinished, incomplete, emerging, and partial (p. 128).

This consideration of what knowledge is conceived to be is fundamental to the valuing of personal professional stories and consequently the role of narratives of experience in professional learning communities. It resonates with the increasing use of narrative as a research methodology, "as a hermeneutic mode of enquiry…which is a question about…how a person makes meaning of some aspect of his or her experience" (Josselson & Lieblich, 1999, p. x). This conceptualisation of open-ended possibility sits well with the complexities of work with young children and invites discussion and debate as part of the social construction of knowledge rather than limiting professional learning to transmission events.

WORKPLACE CHARACTERISTICS

In 1989, Fleet wrote a short piece for *The Australian Journal of Early Childhood* expressing concern about the lack of worth felt by many adults working as early childhood educators, and the steps that might be taken to support these workers. One of the elements identified at that time was the need for administrators and team leaders to recognise the importance of professional development which acknowledges the fundamental humanity of staff members as well as their right to professional growth opportunities. Fifteen years later, in her consideration of a research culture, Yates (2004) commented similarly that, "Conditions in the field may not allow room for practitioners to become involved, [in this case 'in research'] either because of overall workload; or because system arrangements and priorities and constraints change" (p. 172). Stremmel (2002) provided a similar argument and explained that "… few teachers have the time and space in their daily teaching to reflect on what happens in the classroom let alone the resources to document their work and study their own practice" (p. 64). These characteristics of the workplace remain a key element in the growth of effective learning opportunities for early childhood professionals (see also Nuttall, this volume).

In addition to the challenges of appropriate time and space for professional learning, recognition must also be given to the importance of emotionally safe spaces for the risk-taking inherent in personal professional disclosure. There needs to be a collective climate of change resonating in staffrooms and corridors. Individuals are less willing to embark on reflective practice without nurturant colleagues to express interest and join the enterprise.

> Social interaction, engagement in conversation, debate, creative tension, questions, and divergent perspectives among individuals all provoke the development of opinions, understanding, new positions, and professional growth (Potter, 2001, p. 10).

Stonehouse and Gonzales-Mena (2004) refer to this as a "culture of thinking". They claim:

> Adults who work with children need to be people who always want to learn more. It isn't enough just to get together a group of people who have these qualities. In our vision, the workplace nurtures these qualities (p. 175).

This vision of a nurturing environment indicates the extent to which the structural and cultural components of the workplace impact on possibilities for personal, professional learning.

ELEMENTS OF EFFECTIVENESS

The element of ownership as a key principle for professional growth (and indeed educational change) is reflected in Costa and Kallick's (2000) analysis of 'leverage points' for change, or "places within a complex system where a small shift in one condition can produce significant changes throughout the entire system" (p. 12). These leverage points relate to such things as shared vision and goals, school culture, leadership, and the element they refer to as 'continuous learning'. Under this rubric,

> Continuous learning implies an atmosphere of trust, risk-taking, and inquiry. In this sort of atmosphere, data are generated without fear that they will be used to evaluate success or failure. Creativity is also more likely to grow in this type of low-risk environment (ibid, p. 26).

The element of ownership does not presume isolation. On the contrary, it foreshadows a collective of empowered individuals with a belief in the social construction of knowledge. The 'group' not only contributes to its own learning through synergies of circumstance and collective energy, but has the potential of evolving into a critical mass of people who can create a local culture and effect sustainable inquiry.

Jones and Nimmo (1999) note that, "...collaboration that leads to meaningful learning often begins with someone's or something's act of provocation and the willingness of another to become engaged" (p. 6). Nevertheless, there must be a word of caution about open-ended possibilities that float into nothingness, about halting starts and incomplete openings. Scaffolding and closure are as important to narrative as the generation of narrative itself.

Effective professional growth requires systematic engagement in inquiry over time. The power of thinking through one's own dilemmas incorporates both the 'revisiting' of experience in the sense celebrated in Reggio Emilia (Edwards, Gandini & Forman, 1998), and the 'recasting' of experiences in the MacNaughton (2005) sense. Enabling professionals to revisit experiences rather than always moving forward in their practice provides opportunities for personal meaning-making and deeper learning. Groundwater-Smith (1999), reminds us that "there is a difference between having experienced something in the classroom and learning from that experience" (cited in Groundwater-Smith, Ewing, & Le Cornu, 2007, p. 349). Problematising the taken-for-granted and drawing attention to the silences lurking under everyday practices can be transformative, particularly in terms of contextualised decision-making.

An additional element of effectiveness relates directly to the leadership of professional learning. The literature on early childhood leadership highlights the complexity of the role as it applies to diverse responsibilities including centre or site management, personnel development, advocacy and community liaison (Ebbeck & Waniganayake, 2003; Kagan & Bowman, 1997; Rodd, 1998). In terms of leadership, "building a learning community" and "commitment to ongoing professional growth" are noted in a list of effective practices in a major UK study of quality services, (Siraj-Blatchford & Manni, 2006, p. 27). This study also emphasises that being a good leader involves "leading people" and that this is highly context-specific (see also Walker, this volume, and Georgeson, this volume).

Rodd (2006) notes that, "...effective communication in the early childhood context is dependent on the leader's sensitivity to other people's need to feel understood" (p. 71). Being open to and interested in what people 'bring to the table' redefines the role of leaders, those facilitators, provokers, and inspirers who work with those committed to learning. These roles may be performed by one person or contributed by several. Facilitators have a key role in scaffolding experiences as well as providing additional information and resources along the way and assisting closure at key journey points. Having dispensed with the concepts of The Developers and The Developed, such leaders must not only be knowledge-sharers but people-supporters, with an expectation of learning through participation.

REFLECTIONS

For adults and children alike, understanding means being able to develop an interpretive 'theory', a narration that gives meaning to events and objects of the world (Rinaldi, 2006, p. 64).

We have used the device of our storying to construct several narratives. This use of a historicised narrative might be seen as a metaphor for the essence of professional learning, in much the same vein as that presented by Garbett and Tynan (2007), and similarly by Jones and Nimmo (1999):

We are collaborators: we think together, we do workshops together at conferences, we write together. Our book *Emergent curriculum* (1994) is just one testimony to the collaborative engagement we seek from each other (p. 5).

This way of working epitomizes the collegiality associated with working in the early childhood arena, and represents the integrity of contextualized adult learning. We are developing in personally and professionally relevant ways as we work, stretching our boundaries and supporting our investigations of practice rather than being developed by outside development specialists.

Our collegiality also provides a supportive context for what Conle (1996) termed "the subtle workings of experiential narrative exchanges" (p. 310). Such exchanges require the dispositions to trust, to explore as-yet-unknown possibilities, and to accept disequilibrium as an inevitable component of professional reflection. Pursuing such exchanges presumes that the goals of professional growth include strengthening a personal professional knowledge base in conjunction with the social construction of deep learning that informs professional decision-making. This type of learning is separate from acquiring new skills such as using an interactive whiteboard or completing forms to meet funding requirements, pragmatic tasks that are necessary and potentially empowering, but not transformative. These differences in conceptual space need to be considered both by those who are seeking to expand their professional selves and by those who are planning for a workforce to engage effectively in educational change.

REFERENCES

Albrecht, K. M., & Engel, B. (2007). Moving away from a quick-fix mentality to systematic professional development. *Young Children, 62*(4), 18–25.

Abma, T. A. (1999). Powerful stories: The role of stories in sustaining and transforming professional practice within a mental hospital. In R. Josselson & A. Lieblich (Eds.), *Making meaning of narrative. Volume 6 in the narrative study of lives* (pp. 169–195). Thousand Oaks, CA: Sage.

Beattie, M. (1995). New prospects for teacher education: Narrative ways of knowing teaching and teacher learning. *Educational Research, 37*(1), 53–70.

Bruner, J. (2002). *Making stories: Law, literature, life.* New York: Farrar, Straus and Giroux.

Bullough, R. (1993). Case records as personal teaching texts for study in preservice teacher education. *Teaching and Teacher Education, 9*(4), 383–396.

Butt, R., Raymond, D., McCue, G., & Yamagishi, L. (1992). Collaborative autobiography and the teacher's voice. In I. Goodson (Ed.), *Studying teachers' lives* (pp. 51–98). London: Routledge, Kegan Paul.

Carter, K. (1993). The place of story in the study of teaching and teacher education. *Educational Researcher, 22*(1), 5–12.

Chase, S. E. (1995). *Ambiguous empowerment: The work narratives of women school superintendents.* Amherst, MA: University of Massachusetts Press.

Christensen, C., & Hansen, A. (1987). *Teaching and the case method.* Boston: Harvard Business School.

Cole, A., & Knowles, J. G. (1995). Methods and issues in a life-history approach to self-study. In T. Russell & F. Korthagen (Eds.), *Teachers who teach teachers: Reflections on teacher education* (pp. 130–151). London: Falmer Press.

Conle, C. (1996). Resonance in pre-service teacher enquiry. *American Educational Research Journal, 33*(2), 297–325.

Clandinin, D. J., Davies, A., Hogan, P., & Kennard, B. (Eds.). (1993). *Learning to teach, teaching to learn: Stories of collaboration in teacher education.* New York: Teachers College Press.

Connelly, F. M., & Clandinin, D. J. (1998). *Teachers as curriculum planners: Narratives of experience.* New York: Teachers College Press.

Connelly, F. M. & Clandinin, D. J. (1995). Teachers' professional knowledge landscapes: Secret, sacred, and cover stories. In D. J. Clandinin & F. M. Connelly (Eds.), *Teachers' professional knowledge landscapes* (pp. 3–15). New York: Teachers College Press.

Connelly, F. M., & Clandinin, D. J. (1994). Teachers telling stories. *Teacher Education Quarterly, 21*(2), 145–158.

Costa, A. L., & Kallick, B. (2000). Constructing a home for the mind. In A. L. Costa & B. Kallick (Eds.), *Integrating and sustaining habits of mind* (pp. 11–29). Virginia, VA: Association for Supervision and Curriculum Development, in association with Victoria: Hawker Brownlow.

Craig, C. (1995). Dilemmas in crossing the boundaries on the professional knowledge landscape. In D. J. Clandinin & F. M. Connelly (Eds.), *Teachers' professional knowledge landscapes* (pp. 16–24). New York: Teachers College Press.

Czarniawska, B. (2004). *Narratives in social science research.* London: Sage Publications.

Doyle, W. (1990). Case methods in the education of teachers. *Teacher Education Quarterly, 17*(1), 7–15.

Ebbeck, M., & Waniganayake, M. (2003). *Early childhood professionals: Leading today and tomorrow.* NSW: MacLennan & Petty.

Edwards, C., Gandini, L., & Forman, G. (Eds.). (1998). *The hundred languages of children: The Reggio Emilia approach- advanced reflections* (2nd ed.). Connecticut, CT: Ablex.

Fishman, S., & McCarthy, L. (2000). *Unplayed tapes: A personal history of collaborative teacher research.* New York: Teachers College Press.

Fleer, M., & Kennedy, A. (2006). Quality-always unfinished business. In M. Fleer, et al. (Eds.), *Early childhood learning communities: Sociocultural research in practice* (pp. 209–227). NSW: Pearson Education.

Fleet, A. (1989). On being valued as early childhood adults - A note of concern. *Australian Journal of Early Childhood, 14*(4), 3–4.

Fleet, A., & Patterson, C. (1998). Beyond the boxes: Planning for real knowledge and live children. *Australian Journal of Early Childhood, 23*(4), 31–35.

Fleet, A., & Patterson, C. (2002). Changing approaches to planning: Insights into different journeys. *Journal of Research in Early Childhood Education, 9*(1), 1–10.

Fleet, A., & Patterson, C. (2001). Professional growth reconceptualised: Early childhood staff searching for meaning. *Early Childhood Research and Practice, 3*(2). Retrieved October 27, 2008, from http://ecrp.uiuc.edu/v3n2/fleet.html

Fleet, A., Duffie, J., & Patterson, C. (1993). *Early childhood case materials to support the framework of competency standards for the teaching profession.* Final report to National Project on the Quality of Teaching and Learning. Canberra: NPQTL.

Fleet, A., Duffie, J., & Patterson, C. (1995). Capturing the essence of early childhood teaching (K-3) through work-based vignettes. *Australian Research in Early Childhood Education, 1*(1), 82–90.

Fludernik, M. (1996). *Towards a 'Natural' narratology.* London: Routledge.

Garbett, D., & Tynan, B. (2007). Storytelling as a means of reflecting on the lived experience of making curriculum in teacher education. *Australian Journal of Early Childhood, 32*(1), 47–52.

Goodfellow, J., & Hedges, H. (2007). Practitioner research 'centre-stage': Contexts, contributions and challenges. In L. Keesing-Styles & H. Hedges (Eds.), *Theorising early childhood practice: Emerging dialogue* (pp. 187–210). Sydney: Pademelon Press.

Groundwater-Smith, S., Ewing, R., & Le Cornu, R. (2007). *Teaching: Challenges and dilemmas* (3rd ed.). Melbourne: Thomson.

Hargreaves, A., & Fullan, M. (1998). *What's worth fighting for in education?* Buckingham: Open University Press.

Himley, M. (2000). Descriptive inquiry: "Language as a made thing." In M. Himley & P. F. Carini (Eds.), *From another angle: Children's strengths and school standards – the Prospect Center's descriptive review of the child. The practitioner inquiry series* (pp. 126–134). New York: Teachers College Press.

Jalongo, M. J. (1992). Teachers' stories: Our ways of knowing. *Educational Leadership, 49*(7), 68–73.

Jones, E., & Nimmo, J. (1999). Collaboration, conflict, and change: Thoughts on education as provocation. *Young Children, 54*(1), 5–10.

Josselson, R., & Lieblich, A. (1999). *Making meaning of narratives. Volume 6 in the narrative study of lives.* Thousand Oaks, CA: Sage.

Kagan, S., & Bowman, B. (Eds.). (1997). *Leadership in early care and education.* Washington, DC: NAEYC.

MacNaughton, G. (2005). *Doing Foucault in early childhood studies: Applying poststructural ideas.* London: Routledge.

McAninch, A. (1993). *Teacher thinking and the case method: Theory and future directions.* New York: Teachers College Press.

Manning-Morton, J. (2006). The personal is professional: Professionalism and the birth to threes practitioner. *Contemporary Issues in Early Childhood, 7*(1), 42–52.

Martin, W. (1986). *Recent theories of narrative.* Ithaca, NY: Cornell University Press.

Merseth, K. (1991). *The case for cases in teacher education.* Washington, DC: American Association for Higher Education.

Mills, G. (2000). *Action research: A guide for the teacher researcher.* New Jersey, NJ: Prentice Hall.

Nash, C. (1990). *Narrative in culture: The uses of storytelling in the sciences, philosophy, and literature.* London: Routledge.

NSW Department of Community Services. (2002). *NSW curriculum framework for children's services: The practice of relationships.* Sydney: Department of Community Services.

Patterson, C., Fleet, A., & Duffie, J. (Eds.). (1995). *Learning from stories: Early childhood professional experiences.* Sydney: Harcourt Brace.

Patterson, C., & Fleet, A. (1998). Early childhood teachers: Writing to explore professional experience. *Journal of Early Childhood Teacher Education, 19*(1), 71–76.

Patterson, C., & Fleet, A. (1999). Multiple realities: Change in the first years of school. *Journal of Australian Research in Early Childhood Education, 6*(1), 85–97.

Patterson, C., & Fleet, A. (2001). Professional development: Perceptions of relevance. *Journal of Australian Research in Early Childhood Education, 8*(1), 61–70.

Patterson, C., & Fleet, A. (2003). *Meaningful planning: Rethinking teaching and learning relationships.* Canberra: AECA.

Polkinghorne, D. E. (1988). *Narrative knowing and the human sciences.* New York: State University of New York Press.

Potter, G. (2001). The power of collaborative research in teachers' professional development. *Australian Journal of Early Childhood, 26*(1), 8–13.

Richert, A. (1991). Case methods and teacher education: Using cases to teach teacher reflection. In R. Tabachnick & K. Zeichner (Eds.), *Issues and practices in inquiry-oriented teacher education* (pp. 130–150). London: Falmer.

Rinaldi, C. (2006). *In dialogue with Reggio Emilia: Listening researching and learning.* London: Routledge.

Rodd, J. (1998). *Leadership in early childhood: The pathway to professionalism.* NSW: Allen & Unwin.

Rodd, J. (Ed.). (2006). Leadership in early childhood (3rd ed.). Crows Nest, NSW: Allen and Unwin.

Shulman, J. (1991). Revealing the mysteries of teacher-written cases: Opening the black box. *Journal of Teacher Education, 42*(4), 250–262.

Shulman, J. (1992). *Case methods and teacher education.* New York: Teachers College Press.

Siraj-Blatchford, I., & Manni, L. (2006). *Effective Leadership in the Early Years Sector (ELEYS) study.* London: Greater Teaching Council for England.

Stonehouse, A., & Gonzales-Mena, J. (2004). *Making links: A collaborative approach to planning and practice in early childhood services.* NSW: Pademelon Press.

Stremmel, A. (2002). Nurturing professional and personal growth through inquiry. *Young Children, 57*(2), 62–70.

Wassermann, S. (1993). *Getting down to cases: Learning to teach with case studies.* New York: Teachers College Press.

Wenger, E. (1999). *Communities of practice: Learning, meaning and identity.* Boston: Cambridge University Press.

White, H. (1980). The value of narrativity in the representation of reality. *Critical Inquiry, 7*(1), 5–27.

Yates, L. (2004). *What DOES good education research look like?* Berkshire: Open University Press.

Yelland, N. (Ed.). (2005). *Critical issues in early childhood education.* Berkshire: Open University Press.

Alma Fleet,
Institute of Early Childhood,
Macquarie University.
Catherine Patterson
Institute of Early Childhood,
Macquarie University.

MINDY BLAISE

3. REVOLUTIONISING PRACTICE BY DOING EARLY CHILDHOOD POLITICALLY

The Revolutionary Planning Group

INTRODUCTION

This chapter describes how a group of early childhood professionals, who call themselves the Revolutionary Planning Group (RPG) work as a "critically knowing early childhood community (MacNaughton, 2005, p. 188)" to question and reconceptualise taken-for-granted early childhood practices. Drawing from a larger qualitative case study documenting the ongoing work of the RPG, this chapter shows how they are bridging 'major' and 'minor' politics (Dahlberg & Moss, 2005) through collaborative professional learning, in order to generate new pedagogies for their work with children, families, and colleagues. For this chapter, major politics are viewed as larger governmental affairs situated in the wider macro level of society, whereas minor politics happen within the local contexts of early childhood education. The act of linking major and minor politics is considered an example of what I call, 'doing early childhood politically.' How the RPG goes about linking major and minor politics as a critically knowing community and why their activities constitute a distinctive form of professional learning are also discussed.

THE REVOLUTIONARY PLANNING GROUP

Like MacNaughton (2005), Dahlberg and Moss (2005), and others (e.g. Blaise, 2005; Cannella & Viruru, 2004; Grieshaber & Cannella, 2001; Ryan & Grieshaber, 2005; Yelland, 2005), the RPG has been drawing from a range of postmodern perspectives, such as critical theory, feminism, poststructuralism, queer theory, and postcolonialism to understand knowledge, truth, and power differently. These alternative perspectives have been useful for reconceptualising their work with children, families, and colleagues. Influenced by poststructural perspectives, the RPG is questioning knowledge construction. In particular they are interested in reworking the knowledge base of early childhood education by actively resisting dominant discourses that marginalize children, families, and teachers. Discourse is a broad concept referring to a theoretical grid of power and knowledge in which knowledge and power are integrated with each other and impossible to separate (Foucault, 1980a). Discourse is a structuring principle in society (including early

S. Edwards, and J. Nuttall (eds.), Professional Learning in Early Childhood Settings, 27–47.

childhood settings) and language is always located in discourse. When combined with social practices, such as teaching, discourses constitute knowledge, subjectivities, and power relations (Weedon, 1997). Discourse is a way of speaking, writing, thinking, feeling, or doing that incorporates particular ideas as 'truths.' Discourses provide a framework for how we think. They also carry messages about power and seek to establish a set of hidden rules about who has power, what is considered right/normal, and what is considered wrong/abnormal. Power, status, and privilege are constructed through discourse. Some of the discourses found in early childhood include theories of fixed developmental stages as ways of describing children's development; the belief that young children are innocent, naïve, and disconnected from the real world of poverty, racism, or violence; and the assumption that particular families need 'fixing'. These discourses are related to the concept of 'disciplinary power' (Foucault, 1977), which are practices that produce individuals, including children and teachers. Disciplinary power has spread through the production of certain forms of knowledge, such as developmentalism. Disciplinary practices, such as common early childhood observations or traditional ways of working with families, create divisions such as good/bad, healthy/ill, and right/ wrong. Disciplinary power is exercised through these practices and on the bodies and souls of individuals (Sawicki, 1991).

The individual and collective ways in which the RPG is doing early childhood politically is an example of what MacNaughton defines as a "critically knowing early childhood community" (2005, p. 188). MacNaughton imagines professional learning in early childhood designed for change and shares her vision for how early childhood professionals might enact this through critically knowing early childhood communities. MacNaughton is calling for early childhood teachers to engage with current social theories, such as feminism, poststructuralism, postcolonialism, critical and cultural perspectives to inform practice, rather than developmental perspectives. Although the RPG draws from a range of alternative theoretical frameworks to understand their practices differently, they have found poststructuralist perspectives of power and knowledge useful for actively questioning the dominant discourses or 'regimes of truth' (Foucault, 1977) that direct, control, and regulate their practices. Instead of consuming theory, the RPG uses critical thinking to generate new practices based on equity and social justice.

The study

This chapter draws from a larger qualitative case study of how eight early childhood professionals use post-developmental perspectives to generate new pedagogies in their work with children, families, preservice teachers, and colleagues. Over the course of 18 months, seven group meetings and 14 individual interviews have been conducted with participants. Group meetings and individual interviews were audiotaped and transcribed. General interview guides were used to focus these critical and reflexive conversations, which were based on participants' critical engagements with theory, practice, and knowledge production. The interview guides were created from initial analyses of data sources, including field notes from on-site observations, Critical Responses written by four participants, and email exchanges between all participants. These Critical Responses involved participants formally and individually responding to a current topic or issue presented to the group. Some topics that were presented included how they perceived developmental perspectives or the role of the RPG in their particular work environments. Artefacts that were collaboratively created, including program planning formats, philosophy statements, professional development workshop plans, and *The Manifesto* (Revolutionary Planning Group, 2004; see Appendix A) were also part of the data set.

Overall, the study was an attempt to document and support the various ways that these early childhood professionals collaboratively generate and theorize early childhood practices and knowledge. Instead of objectifying practice and what these professionals are (or are not) doing, this project attempted to support their roles as knowledge generators while the group researched, theorised, interpreted, and critiqued theoretical perspectives, curriculum, policies, and traditional early childhood practices (Cochran-Smith & Lytle, 1993). The nature of this support varied between formal and informal practices by myself and participants. I provided formal support by supplying academic readings that showed how early childhood teachers were challenging developmental discourses or through planned questions that aimed to encourage critical reflection. Informal support occurred amongst the RPG members through listening, encouragement, and working together on projects. It is through this work that the RPG is learning how to challenge normative practices. As a result they are constantly in the process of taking a stance and doing early childhood politically by critically engaging with major politics, different perspectives, practices, and each other. I argue that this constitutes a distinctive form of continuing professional learning generated organically by a group of committed professionals.

The participants

The Revolutionary Planning Group (RPG) is made up of eight early childhood professionals who are working for equity and social justice across diverse settings and contexts in Victoria, Australia. Although all participants have worked directly with young children as early childhood teachers, some are currently involved in the field of early childhood education as teacher educators, policy officers, managers, or coordinators of kindergarten clusters. Although I have taken-on the role of the researcher for this project, I am also considered to be a member of the RPG. Currently I am an academic in early childhood education. My career as an early childhood professional began in the USA, where I taught kindergarten (5 and 6-year-olds) and second grade (7 and 8-year-olds) in public elementary schools. I have been an early childhood teacher educator and researcher in Australia, Singapore, and the USA. My researching and teaching interests focus on the possibilities of using alternative theoretical perspectives to inform practice.

Three of the participants, Maree, Denise, and Yarrow, work directly with young children as early childhood teachers. Denise and Maree are both qualified kindergarten teachers working in socioeconomically disadvantaged and culturally diverse contexts. Both Denise and Maree have been recipients of national and state-wide teaching awards. For example, in 2007 Denise won the National Excellence in Teaching Award (NEiTA) and Maree received a Victorian Education Excellence Award and was named the Outstanding Early Childhood Teacher Award in 2008 by the Department of Education and Early Childhood Development. Yarrow, who has worked as a qualified kindergarten teacher in sessional kindergarten and in long day care, is currently the head teacher in the babies' room at a university-based childcare centre.

Brian, Anne, Debbie, and Catharine are the remaining members of the RPG. Although Brian began his early childhood career over 30 years ago as one of the first male kindergarten teachers in New Zealand, he is at present the Manager of Children's Services at a large university. Anne recently left kindergarten teaching to become a kindergarten cluster management coordinator across several early childhood centres in Melbourne, Australia. Debbie is the manager of the children's program at a demonstration centre in Melbourne. Catharine is the Early Years Strategy Project Manager for a large non-profit organization. She is responsible for the development of key projects to enhance the organization's research and advocacy agenda for young children and their families living in disadvantage.

Collectively, the group has a rich and complex history and over the years their personal, professional, and political lives have overlapped. Debbie and Denise met approximately 15 years ago while working at the same childcare centre. Although Yarrow and Brian knew each other through their past involvement in the Research Action Network for Gender Equity (RANGE), they now find themselves at the same workplace. Anne and Maree met Brian, Yarrow, and Denise at a national early childhood conference, where they discovered that they shared similar interests and questions around programming and planning. I met Yarrow and Brian in Australia when I was invited to present at an early childhood conference and we discovered that we had similar interests about gender and sexuality. As a result of of these shared interests, Yarrow and I have collaborated on several research projects (see Andrew & Blaise, 2008; Blaise & Andrew, 2005). Since these meetings, the RPG has presented at conferences about why and how they have been revolutionising their practices. The level of political activism of these group members is considerable, and can be traced back to the late 1970's, with Brian's involvement in the National Childcare Campaign and the Lambeth Community Under Fives Campaign in England. More recently, Catharine, Brian, and Denise have been involved in advocacy groups such as Real Rights for Refugee Children (Newman, 2005) and Denise and Anne led their kindergartens' participation in the SIEVX National Memorial Project[1].

MAJOR AND MINOR POLITICS

'Major' and 'minor' politics are ideas that Dahlberg and Moss (2005) explore in their book, *Ethics and Politics in Early Childhood Education*. They draw from the works of Rose (1999) and Delueze and Guatarri (1999) who write about the important part that politics plays in everyday life. For Deleuze and Guatarri (ibid) "...everything is political, but every politics is simultaneously *macropolitics* and a *microprolitics*" (p. 213). If everything is political, then the pedagogies that teachers use in their everyday work in the classroom, ranging from what books to include in the reading corner to how (or if) group time happens, can be considered examples of minor politics. Additionally, Rose (ibid) argues that minor politics happens in the here and now, and are based on small and immediate concerns. For Rose, minor politics are modest and pragmatic actions that have a critical attitude. Major politics are viewed as larger governmental affairs situated in the wider macro level of society. The practices of the RPG include both micro and macro politics.

The group meetings the RPG had were much more than just teachers getting together and talking about practice. Instead, they can be considered examples of critical inquiry. Critical inquiry is a "process of systematic, rigorous and critical reflection about professional practice, and the contexts in which it occurs, in ways that question taken-for-granted assumptions" (Reid, 2004, p. 4). Inquiries can be thought of as catalysts for changing practices. These inquiries become critical when the reflections and actions are linked to larger ethical, social, and political issues.

As a form of critical inquiry the work of the RPG is related to macro politics. This is evident in several of the RPG's collective activities, such as *The Wheel of Beliefs* and *The Manifesto*. The following section describes how the RPG's interest in contesting developmentalism has been an ongoing project beginning with the creation of *The Wheel of Beliefs* to their more recent development of *The Manifesto*. These are two examples of how collaborative tools help the RPG actively link major and minor politics to do early childhood politically.

Contesting developmentalism

A core interest for the group is contesting dominant discourses, or 'regimes of truth' (Foucault, 1977) that constitute early childhood education. Developmentalism is one of the dominant discourses that shapes and constructs curriculum, planning, environments, and practices. The RPG's interest in questioning developmentalism has built over time and their initial inquiries about developmental perspectives were based on concerns that members had with curriculum programming and planning. Several members were becoming frustrated with the technicist practices of program planning, which valued one way of understanding children, learning, and teaching. They felt traditional ways of documenting children's learning focused on developmental domains that could be universally determined and neatly recorded. They were also concerned that documentation of children's learning tended to focus on and highlight what children could not do, rather than what they could do. In short, it was a deficit-based, rather than a strength-based approach to planning. Several group members wondered if the observations that they were expected 'to do on children' even focused on children's learning at all. Maree shared her dissatisfaction with this way of working with children when she commented how so much of planning was about the future, rather than valuing the 'now' and how the 'now' is important to children and the adults that she works with (Critical Response, 2006). Maree's critique is showing how the dominant conventions of observation and documentation shape policies, practices, and relationships in particular ways. It was this concern about these particular ways of understanding children, learning, and teaching that encouraged the RPG to not only discuss and debate the 'truths' of early childhood education, but also to rework their practices. In this way, the RPG began to create their own agenda, one of critique and experimentation, for their ongoing learning about their teaching practices.

The practicing early childhood teachers in the group all felt they were planning just to meet the requirements of the Department of Education and Early Childhood Development[2]. They also believed that their planning never seemed to match the ways they engaged with children. Anne began to see how this kind of planning is a form of surveillance or technologies of normalization (Foucault, 1980a) when she commented on how planning was primarily about, "showing you're doing your job. You know, showing that lovely things happened" (Group meeting, 2006). When planning becomes a strategy for accountability and in this case for providing evidence that Anne was providing 'lovely' experiences for children, this becomes a technique for constructing norms or truths in practice. For the RPG, this way of constructing childhood and teaching was limiting, biased, and oppressive.

The RPG's concerns with developmentalism are situated within wider critiques of the field's overreliance of developmental psychology to influence practice (see Cannella, 1997; Fleer, 1995; Hatch, et al., 2002; Kessler & Swadener, 1992; Lubeck, 1998; Mallory & New, 1994; Ryan & Grieshaber, 2005 and Yelland, 2005). These initial concerns about developmentalism can be traced to everyday classroom practices, specifically while group members were teaching. For example, Brian first began questioning developmentalism while working with preservice early childhood teachers as a teacher in vocational education. When asked how he first realised the limitations of child development, Brian responded:

> ...the frustrations about the developmental stuff I think came from reading ideas, but more from going and assessing students on placement and reading endless observations and checklists about children when I was in the room watching and then realising that all of that information didn't tell me much about those children (Interview, 2006).

Because of his dissatisfaction with preservice teachers' observations of children, Brian began asking them to tell him more about the children they were working with, particularly what they were like as people. He would ask the preservice teachers, "Well, tell me about these kids. What are they like?" By asking questions that are not usually found on the developmental forms students (and teachers) are required to complete, Brian realised the limitations of the checklists. In particular, he noticed how they failed to capture the qualities that make people unique and create who we are, such as gender, 'race,' class, or sexuality. For Brian, the checklists create (and maintain) adult perceptions of what children should be. With apprehension Brian stated:

Oh the idea just of continually measuring the abnormal is limiting and a huge amount of work [by the preservice teachers] went into building these developmental profiles of children.....and these profiles render a whole lot of that social stuff invisible. So stuff around gender in particular, sort of disappeared off the agenda because it sort of didn't fit into the boxes (Interview, 2006).

Brian is learning that developmentalism fails to privilege or recognize children's identities. Similarly, Dahlberg, Moss, and Pence (1999) explore the ways that developmental psychology produces an image of the child as scientifically natural, rather than socially, culturally, and dynamically constructed. A developmental construction of children fails to recognize the importance of children's identities and the active role that young children take in constructing themselves as gendered, 'raced,' classed, or sexual beings (Blaise, 2005). Consequently, developmental profiles do not include such aspects of children, or if they do, they are treated as biologically determined and fixed facts, rather than socially constructed and full of contradictions, multiplicities, shifts, and changes.

When asking the RPG to reflect on when and how the group collectively began questioning developmentalism, Brian shares how he, Denise, and Yarrow would problematize their beliefs about teaching and learning. They would often sit around Brian's kitchen table, talking about political events and how this was making its way into their professional lives. As Fleet and Patterson argue (Chapter 2, this volume) the practice of sharing professional narratives, and of developing collective narratives of practice, in itself provides a valuable form of ongoing professional learning. Through sharing accounts of their experiences, Brian, Denise, and Yarrow soon realised there was a mismatch between what they believed about children and learning, and the role of the early childhood teacher. They began noticing how developmental discourses constructed what they did and did not do in the classroom. At first, it was the assumptions of developmentalism and how it was enacted in written forms that they began to notice and challenge. It was this recognition of the power and knowledge of written documentation that was a catalyst for the RPG to change how they were conducting observations of children's learning.

The Wheel of Beliefs

For Brian, a whole new "layer of energy" happened when Denise and Yarrow started articulating how their ideas and philosophies clashed with traditional notions of early childhood teaching. Brian said,

We started documenting our ideas onto paper and eventually Yarrow made it into reality when he created this large *Wheel of Beliefs*. The large wooden wheel showed how we were expanding the usual social, emotional, cognitive, and physical domains of development to now include aspects such as self-respect, self-discipline, food appreciation, sexuality, etc. (Interview, 2006)

33

This *Wheel of Beliefs* represents one attempt to decentre and undermine developmentalism and privilege other ideas about children. Although the *Wheel of Beliefs* was originally created and used by all of the staff at the childcare centre where Yarrow was employed as a kindergarten teacher, it showed how adults were thinking differently about children. During a professional development day, Yarrow asked all of the staff, ranging from the cook to the director, to generate a list of what they (not child development) really valued about children. According to Yarrow, "It freed us up. Everybody started seeing children differently." The RPG used the *Wheel of Beliefs* to question and dismantle the regimes of developmental truth in early childhood. Not only were they learning about the flaws and politics of developmentalism, but they were also learning how they could challenge this particular way of 'knowing' children. The *Wheel of Beliefs* is just one of several artefacts created by the RPG in order to contest developmentalism.

The Manifesto

Over time the RPG became increasingly frustrated with the normalising practices and discourses of developmentalism. The group began meeting regularly and engaged in various forms of critical discussions about programming and planning. Usually this involved one member describing a practice related to programming and then the group interrogating the assumptions and beliefs about learning and teaching upon which the practice was based. However, these meetings were not just about critiquing; they became a catalyst for doing early childhood differently and politically. For instance, one group meeting was used to construct *The Manifesto* (Revolutionary Planning Group, 2004, see Appendix A). This working document represents the values and beliefs the RPG has for the field of early childhood education. While debating and constructing *The Manifesto*, the group decided to name themselves the RPG. Reflecting on the naming of the RPG, Brian recalled:

> I think it was Yarrow's idea and it was deliberately designed to provoke. It was to sit against the 'nice ladies' idea, to provoke the sector into action, and to challenge perceptions of early childhood as safe and comfortable (Critical Response, 2007).

It is not just the naming of the RPG that was deliberate; the creation of The Manifesto was also intended to provoke debate and discussion. The Manifesto is the RPG's attempt to articulate a new vision for the field of early childhood education, reifying an alternative perspective about children and teaching. It was also meant to encourage debate about what is and is not happening in the field of early childhood. Unintentionally, The Manifesto has served as a tool that supports the risky business of doing teaching politically.

For Anne, who has recently left teaching to co-ordinate the management of a group (known in Victoria as a 'cluster') of kindergartens, *The Manifesto* has been useful for engaging in conversations with the kindergarten teachers she was meeting in her new role. She explained:

The Manifesto is an extremely empowering document for me. I refer to it constantly, sometimes as a document in itself, but more often than not by voicing its essence to other early childhood professionals in conversation, informally and formally. However, I realise many of its 10 points are now so embedded in my philosophy as an educator, that *The Manifesto* has become the catalyst for the conversations I am having (Critical Response, 2007).

For Brian, *The Manifesto* supported the changes that have occurred at one of the children's services he manages in how the program is planned and evaluated. For example:

Moving away from observations, checklists, and wall plans to interest-based programming, journals, and photographs have really inspired and encouraged staff. And the way it has evolved there—a big centre with six rooms—is that it's not done one way. Every group does it slightly differently, it's ever changing, and people really think about what they're doing. The variety really excites me as it moves away from the idea of one answer, but also gives space for teachers' own ideas and creativity to emerge more strongly (Critical Response, 2007).

For these early childhood professionals, the RPG supports the risky business of doing early childhood teaching politically. It is evident that this work is not just about critiquing the knowledges of early childhood education, rather it is also about knowledge production. *The Manifesto* might be considered both an *example* of how new knowledge is constructed through critical inquiries and doing teaching politically, and as a *tool* for ongoing the construction of ideas and practice, within a critically knowing early childhood community. As a critically knowing early childhood community, the RPG has learned how to contest the dominant discourses of early childhood, opening up possibilities for change and transformation. In turn, these actions enable the RPG to revolutionise early childhood teaching, making it possible to reverse the trend toward the deskilling of teachers and the "stupidification" of students (Kincheloe, 2003, p. 19).

DOING EARLY CHILDHOOD POLITICALLY

A closer look at *The Manifesto* and how these ideals are enacted in practice is useful for exploring how the RPG is doing early childhood politically. *The Manifesto* itself shows how the RPG is aware of major politics. For instance the first statement of *The Manifesto* reads, "Indigenous culture should be central to all early childhood services." The RPG intentionally placed this statement first in *The Manifesto* to make a political point about the importance of Indigenous culture and issues in early childhood. As Brian explained,

It is important and significant that it [Indigenous culture] is first on *The Manifesto* as to me it represents our grounding or starting point. This is in part inspired by work in Aotearoa New Zealand where the Tiriti o Waitangi[3] is the foundation of the nation, and spelled out in Te Whariki (their early childhood curriculum framework) and genuinely seen by many in the field as a very real and realisable obligation to that country's first people (Critical Response, 2007).

Politics creates opportunities for seeing things differently and for challenging the status quo. The RPG has been rethinking the role of the early childhood teacher from one that conforms to traditional practices towards one that is transforming knowledge and power (MacNaughton, 2003). Although it may not be easy to generate new discourses about early childhood teaching, it is not impossible. Instead of attempting to challenge and change the entire field of early childhood education, Foucault recommends (1980b) focusing on the local sites that we work in and finding ways to resist disciplinary power that produces certain forms of knowledge. This perspective makes the early childhood classroom a potential site for resistance and change. By paying attention to the interplay between learning within the group and changes in practice, we can see how the concept of minor politics (exemplified in *The Manifesto*) has provoked powerful professional learning for group members. For example, the ways Yarrow encouraged his colleagues, including the cook, teaching assistants, and director to understand children differently is one way an early childhood community resisted develop-mental discourses. The *Wheel of Beliefs* was produced first with the RPG and then reworked within the childcare centre and supported changed practices amongst staff. This is an attempt to produce different kinds of knowledge about children.

Field notes showed that all of the practitioners displayed Indigenous artefacts in their centres (i.e., Indigenous flags, handprints, Indigenous puzzles, and books) and engaged with difficult Indigenous issues. For instance, observations of Yarrow's teaching showed how he Acknowledged Country with the children in his program. Acknowledging Country is a symbolic gesture of reconciliation where a speaker opens an event by acknowledging that it is taking place on the traditional country of the Indigenous community. It is a practice that can take place even when traditional elders are not present. Yarrow has modified a practice, which is usually saved for public events, such as the opening of a conference or a new childcare centre, to include children. On a small table, located near the entryway to the kindergarten room, stood a medium-sized black candle, a small Indigenous flag, some eucalyptus leaves, and Dick Roughsey's (1975) children's book, *The Rainbow Serpent*. Standing with a small group of children around the table, Yarrow lit the candle while saying, "Before going out to play, we would like to acknowledge the Wurundjerri people, who are the original owners of the land that we play on." The children that were gathered around Yarrow seemed to be genuinely interested in this daily ritual as they watched Yarrow light the candle. It seemed as though Yarrow and the children were meaningfully engaged in that moment of Acknowledging Country.

Another example of how the RPG interacts with Indigenous culture and issues was observed when Maree invited Aunty Lillian, an Australian Aboriginal Elder, to visit her kindergarten and speak about the Aboriginal flag and what it means. Aunty Lillian told the children how the red colour in the flag represents blood that has been spilt over land and rights. After she left, the children were curious about the violence and the blood and wanted to know why blood was spilt, who was killed, and why. Although Maree found these conversations difficult, she chose not to shy away from the children's questions because she knew it was an important and necessary discussion to have, because what is going on in the wider community (the macro politics) influences these children.

Although some adults might consider raising Indigenous issues with young children as insignificant, the RPG thinks differently. Like other early childhood teachers who reflect on the ways the early childhood curriculum enables and limits how children construct Indigenous and non-Indigenous identities (e.g., Cave, King, & Guigini, 2005; MacNaughton & Davis, 2001), the RPG recognizes the necessity for addressing indigeneity. Highlighting Indigenous issues in early childhood is important and fundamental because it is a central fact in Australian history that Indigenous culture has been oppressed. Like Maree, Yarrow is committed to integrating these issues into his practice because he is aware of "...colonialism and the marginalisation and silencing of minority discourses, not only within Australian history, but within the field of early childhood" (Interview, 2007). Both Maree and Yarrow are linking major and minor politics into the everyday work they do. These are examples of how early childhood teachers are practicing politically.

Taking action and doing early childhood politically, either individually or collectively, is important to the RPG and they are interested in revolutionising the field of early childhood education by changing their everyday practices. They view their local settings as productive sites for doing early childhood otherwise. For the RPG, it is necessary to do more than just question the dominant discourses of early childhood. Rather, they see the importance of grappling with difficult social and political issues, taking them on board, and then trying out new ways of critically engaging with children, families, and colleagues.

According to Dahlberg and Moss (2005) minor politics opens up new spaces to do things differently in early childhood. Although minor politics can take many forms, the main features include critical thinking, contesting knowledge, and constructing new knowledges. By doing early childhood politically, members of the RPG are contesting knowledge and constructing new ways of working within early childhood communities. The following section explores how one of the RPG members, Maree is doing early childhood politically. Maree is thinking critically about engaging with families, contesting traditional ways for involving parents in early childhood settings, and constructing new knowledge about early childhood teaching. By bridging major and minor politics, Maree is learning about the political nature of teaching and transforming her practices in order to challenge social injustices. Maree's learning and actions also demonstrate the close relationship between risk-taking and professional learning; in order to learn, Maree risks new practices, which may or may not succeed.

MAREE'S MINOR POLITICS: REWORKING RELATIONSHIPS

Maree is the lead kindergarten teacher and director of a local council kindergarten in one of Victoria's most economically disadvantaged areas. For the past three years Maree has recognised that traditional ways of including families, such as having a parent committee, asking parents to help with morning tea, or having social nights at the kindergarten does not work in her context. Maree's minor politics can be seen in the ways she is reworking her relationships with families. Maree claims that taking risks and understanding the complexities of relationships is important to why and how she changes her practices. She has learned that staying with 'safe' early childhood practices does not always support the children and families at her kindergarten. When asked about the families that use the kindergarten service, Maree said:

> Many families live in Ministry of Housing accommodation. There are lots of children from single parent families and families who face long term unemployment. There are also a lot of children who are in the care of the state or whose families are involved with child protection agencies. Many of the children are from Culturally And Linguistically Different (CALD) backgrounds. [This part of Melbourne] has a large population of families from Somalia and we have many children from this background and from other parts of the world, so displacement of families is a significant issue (Critical Response, 2006).

The families Maree encounters at her service are directly influenced by issues associated with globalization (Yelland & Kilderry, 2005; Robinson & Diaz, 2006), yet the traditional ways that early childhood teachers are expected to work with families does not always take their social, political, and cultural contexts into consideration.

Hughes and MacNaughton (1999) explored the politics of knowledge that underpins the dominant discourses of parent-teacher relationships in early childhood education. Their analysis of 162 items published in the 1990's that focused on parent involvement as their key concern revealed that parental knowledge is most often viewed as inadequate, supplementary, or unimportant, rather than necessary, viable, and valuable. These dominant discourses about families and how early childhood encourages teachers to include parents, trouble Maree. She explained:

> There's this traditional way of thinking that children come to kindergarten with nothing else happening in their lives and this does not take into account all the things that impact on children's lives outside of here [kindergarten]. I'm trying to look at what I can do to help support families and develop relationships, especially when we don't have a parent committee and we don't have the traditional milk and fruit roster. Traditional ways of having social nights don't work in this setting as families don't come out at night. So, developing relationships has to work in other ways (Critical Response, 2006).

Although Maree sees the importance of developing relationships with families, she recognizes that they are complex, unpredictable, and at times contentious. Maree understands these complexities by recognizing major politics and how they influence the families using the kindergarten services. In her attempt to understand these complexities, Maree takes risks in her practice. For Maree, 'risky business' is her willingness to explore some of those harder aspects of teaching, such as not always being certain about how these relationships will develop or at having the 'right' answer.

Minor political practices

Five minor political practices that Maree uses in her everyday context for reworking relationships with families include greeting families, rethinking time, valuing different kinds of relationships, the sign-in book, and the sewing circle. As minor political practices they are aimed at challenging the status quo or the ways teachers usually work with families. They might also be considered subversive acts, intended to disrupt normative ways that some teachers work with families in early childhood settings.

Greeting families

Maree tries to ensure all families feel welcomed in the kindergarten service by greeting them each day. When describing this practice, Maree said:

> Something we want families to feel is that sense of belonging. So we've worked really hard to do that, to try and make sure that families do feel welcome and that we make sure we try and talk to each family. So everyone has a different relationship and how they choose to be a part of the centre is important (Interview, 2006).

Instead of recognizing and saying good morning to the child who takes part in the kindergarten program or giving a quick smile to the parent who has dropped off their child for kindergarten, Maree acknowledges that children are part of families in the ways she greets them when they arrive. Therefore, "...we greet you [the child] as part of your family and we value your family" (Interview, 2006). For Maree, this practice of purposively engaging with children and their parents together, when they enter the kindergarten, is her way of recognizing and letting everyone know the family is important and valued. It is also about working towards letting children know she sees them as a significant part of their families. Greeting families takes time and it has required Maree to rethink how she physically embodies teaching. She explains, "...rather than sitting at the drawing table and not moving, and making everyone come to you, we go there" (Interview, 2006). This is an example of how minor political practices include small, but significant, changes in the ways Maree physically engages with and greets families.

Rethinking the importance of time

Observations in Maree's classroom revealed her warmly greeting families as they arrive at the kindergarten, regardless of the time. That is, greeting families does not only happen at the beginning of the kindergarten session, because many of the children and their families do not arrive until well after it begins. On several occasions, Maree mentioned the practice of arriving on time. She particularly focussed on how most teachers emphasize the importance of children arriving on time to kindergarten. As Maree builds relationships with families, she finds out about their lives and why this is not always easy. Most of this information has forced her to rethink the role of the kindergarten program and what she values. Not only has she become more flexible in what she views as important, but she is letting go of 'good teaching' myths that serve to maintain inequitable power relationships. For Maree, it no longer matters if children arrive to kindergarten an hour (or three) after the session begins. Instead, it is more important that families and children come. Maree's attitude about when children come to kindergarten is very different from how most early childhood teachers think about this practice. This was reflected when Catharine commented on the first time she met Maree at a professional in-service session. Catharine remembers several attendees claiming that for children who only come for the last half hour of the session, "…they don't get anything out of it" (Group meeting, 2006). Catharine went on to explain how Maree provided a counter-narrative to these teachers' views about when children arrive and for how long they participate in the session:

> Now Maree had completely the opposite view of it and it was less about the time and when you were *meant* to be there and more about the relationship that she was building with the families. She kept saying, "Whenever you get here, however you come, it will be about us forming a relationship. Even if you are feeling shitty when you get here, it will still be okay. You're still welcome. You're accepted. It doesn't matter. Stay for half an hour. Stay for ten minutes. You know, you might come back for ten minutes tomorrow, but you know, we are here. And whatever the experience of the session will be it doesn't mean to say that you get the best part of the session when you come at 9 o'clock or if you come at eleven thirty. But you know, whenever you get here is when you get here" (Group meeting, 2006).

For many of the Somali families who are refugees and do not have extended families living in Australia, getting their youngest children to the kindergarten for the beginning of the session is difficult. Maree said, "…[I]t doesn't matter when they come….because they don't have an extended support network….and they're the mums. They are the ones responsible for getting all of the children to school" (Group meeting, 2006). This acknowledgement that families might have difficulties getting to kindergarten 'on time' has challenged Maree to rethink what she values as an early childhood teacher, and getting to the kindergarten session on time is no longer high on Maree's list of priorities for families.

Valuing different kinds of relationships

Maree also talked about how she and the staff have different relationships with different families. She recognizes that some families are easier to engage with than others. Often, the difficulty is because some families don't want to talk through issues or concerns. Although this makes it hard to establish relationships with some families, those families shouldn't be ignored. Maree recognizes what is really important is that she, "…rises to get to know families…. For some [families] it can be a hello and goodbye. But for others it is very different. Especially for those who are angry with the world or upset" (Group meeting, 2006). Accepting that not all relationships with families will be the same or 'great' goes against traditional ways of thinking about working with others in early childhood. That is, often teachers aim to treat everyone as being the same or equal, rather than taking an equity perspective (Blaise, 2006). An equity perspective attempts to recognize the historical, cultural, and political histories of others, rather than assuming that everyone (children, families, and colleagues) comes to the classroom with similar experiences, expectations, and needs.

Maree also believes that by accepting the different kinds of relationships she has with families, she must also acknowledge that families will choose to participate in a variety of ways with the kindergarten. Again, teachers' thinking about how families 'should' be engaging with the early childhood community is often not the reality of how families actually choose to participate, for various reasons. Maree's way of thinking about these relationships is a strategy for recognizing that for some families, the contexts they are part of influence their lives in ways that early childhood has not always thoughtfully recognized or known how to negotiate.

The sign-in book

A fourth micro political practice Maree has developed to build relationships with families is the way she uses the sign-in book for encouraging families to linger and stay a while at the kindergarten. In Victoria, all kindergartens are required to show evidence of families using early childhood services and these records are usually kept in a sign-in book. Maree has played with the sign-in book by strategically moving it around the room. This practice requires families to 'come in' and stay a while in the kindergarten. With a laugh, Maree shared how it has become sort of a game with the families. She said,

> When the signing-in book goes further down the room, they'll [families] often have a bit of a laugh that I've moved it. Sometimes when they can't find it immediately, they actually have to linger longer in a different part of the kinder. After they find the book, I've noticed how they take a few minutes to look around that area of the kinder (Interview, 2006).

This 'game' has played a significant role transforming the relationships she has with some families. Moving the book around the room and providing the families with an informal game, which requires them to physically come into the classroom and find the sign-in book, has helped shift the power relationships between Maree and some families. For instance, this game has encouraged families to engage with Maree when they arrive and seems to make them feel more comfortable and welcomed in the classroom. Again, Maree is recognizing how these families might

41

need different kinds of support for establishing and maintaining relationships. For example:

It's just looking at those ways of trying to build relationships with families and I think sometimes that if a family comes in and they're not with their child because she or he has found a friend to play with, sometimes it's hard for them to begin a conversation because they don't always know what to say (Interview, 2006).

Sewing circle

At the beginning of the year, Maree asked the families what kinds of activities they would like to do. They were not interested in a formalized parenting program. Instead they showed an interest in more social activities like sewing and going to the movies together. Maree views these social activities as positive because they provide opportunities for families to develop relationships with each other and, hopefully, these friendships will allow them to support each other about parenting practices. This is a very different approach towards parenting programs. The more traditional way, where the kindergarten organizes a parent educator to come and talk to parents, positions parental knowledge as insufficient. In contrast, Maree tried organizing a sewing circle that would make space for the grandmothers or mums to talk with one another in an informal setting. This would allow the women to sit off to the side sewing in the kindergarten, talking with each other while also watching their children play. Not only would this allow them opportunities to meet other adults who might not be a part of their immediate social networks, it also lets them see and talk about their children participating in the kindergarten program. Maree recognizes that these families have a lot of knowledge amongst themselves about parenting and they in turn can support one another, rather than being told by a parenting 'expert' how to raise their children.. Although Maree did not consider the sewing circle to be a success and found sustaining it difficult, it is important to recognize that this practice was an attempt to facilitate contacts between families, or helping to create networks of support (Keyser, 2006).

Although these strategies for building relationships with families may seem simple, they are actually highly complex and potentially problematic. Maree confronts these relationships head on, even if the consequences are messy, rather than trying to shoe-horn families into dominant early childhood discourses. For Maree, building relationships with families is about getting to know their customs and then incorporating them in ways that are meaningful into the program. For example, knowing that the majority of the families she works with are Muslim, she ensures that the food is Halal and non-Christian customs are valued in the kindergarten. Even so, at times this has been difficult. It is the values that families hold about education and learning that are sometimes harder to navigate than the inclusion of customs and traditions. For instance, it is enormously important for the Muslim families that their children are able to attend the local Islamic primary school. However, in order to attend this school, children must pass a formal readiness test. Again, this has challenged Maree to rethink the role of the kindergarten program and change some of her practices in order to create learning pathways that support children to prepare for this test.

As a member of the RPG, Maree contributes by sharing her dilemmas and her emerging minor political practices. The RPG is then able to challenge Maree further as she continues to rework her relationships with families. It is through this individual and collaborative work that Maree is bridging major and minor politics and doing early childhood politically. Furthermore, in de-privatising the relationship between action and reflection-on-action in collaboration with other RPG members, Maree is highly accountable for her ongoing learning and practice.

REVOLUTIONIZING PROFESSIONAL LEARNING

As a critically knowing early childhood community, the RPG is constantly doing early childhood politically. Their work is made up of continuous and intentional back-and-forth learning as they move between major and minor politics, micro and macro contexts, critical thinking and action, and the RPG collective and individual early childhood contexts. This back-and-forth negotiation is a key component to the RPG's professional learning. Not only do members of the RPG support the critical work of each other, but they are constantly interrogating each others practice. For instance, when Maree was reworking her relationships with families she would come to RPG meetings and share her revolutionary practices. This involved discussing Australia's current refugee policies, how racism was surfacing across the continent, and how families were marginalized within early childhood services. The RPG took these political issues on board, rather than declaring them inappropriate or insignificant for early childhood.

Another example of how the RPG revolutionized their professional learning is evident in how they learned to move between micro and macro contexts of early childhood. This is evident in how the RPG used the *Wheel of Beliefs* and *The Manifesto*. Although both the *Wheel of Beliefs* and *The Manifesto* are different examples of contesting developmental discourses, one was used primarily with teachers and the other was intended for the wider field of early childhood education. The *Wheel of Beliefs* challenged local early childhood communities to plan differently for and with children, whereas *The Manifesto* speaks to the major politics of what the RPG believes the field of early childhood education should be.

These inquiries into practice revolutionize professional learning because the RPG is reworking practice politically. What makes the RPG different from other critically knowing early childhood communities is the combination of their histories, political activism, and critical engagements with macro and micro politics. Their personal, professional, and political lives are uniquely intertwined, individually and collectively. Their constant and somewhat organic back-and-forth activities make their professional learning revolutionary. It also makes their learning impossible to replicate; whilst other groups of early childhood educators could form similar groups, the learning that results is bound to be highly idiosyncratic. If there is not a 'right' or singular way to do early childhood politically, then revolutionizing professional learning is also context specific. This is just one example of how a group of early childhood professionals are revolutionizing learning and teaching. Their stories of doing early childhood politically are important and might inspire others to create new and different ways for engaging with macro politics in order to create minor political practices that both challenge the status quo and generate new knowledges.

NOTES

[1] SIEVX National Memorial Project was a controversial 'people's memorial' to the 353 people who drowned on the refugee boat SIEVX on the 20th, October 2001 (see www.sievxmemorial.com for more information about the project).

[2] The Department of Education and Early Childhood Development (DEECD) is responsible for regulating the delivery of children's services in the state of Victoria.

[3] Tiriti o Waitangi is the treaty first signed on 6th February 1840 by representatives of the British Crown and various Maori chiefs. It established a British governor in New Zealand, recognised Maori ownership of their lands, and gave Maori the rights of British subjects.

REFERENCES

Andrew, Y., & Blaise, M. (2008). The impact of men on young children's play. *Every Child, 14*(2), 15.

Blaise, M. (2005). *Playing it straight!: Uncovering gender discourses in the early childhood classroom*. New York: Routledge.

Blaise, M. (2006). Those who are in, those who are out, and those who are seldom seen, In G. Latham, M. Blaise, S. Dole, J. Faulkner, J. Lang, & K. Malone (Eds.), *Learning to teach: New times, new practices* (pp. 66–95). Victoria, Australia: Oxford University Press.

Blaise, M., & Andrew, Y. (2005). How 'bad' can it be?: Troubling gender, sexuality, and early childhood teaching. In N. Yelland (Ed.), *Critical issues in early childhood education* (pp. 49–57). Berkshire, England: Open University Press.

Cannella, G. S. (1997). *Deconstructing early childhood education: Social justice and revolution*. New York: Peter Lang.

Cannella, G. S., & Viruru, R. (2004). *Childhood and postcolonization: Power, education, and contemporary practice*. New York: RoutledgeFalmer.

Cave, L., King, S. J., & Guigni, M. (2005). Chromatics: A whiter shade of pink. *International Journal of Equity and Innovation in Early Childhood, 3*(1), 31–49.

Cochran-Smith, M., & Lytle, S. L. (1993). *Inside/outside: Teacher research and knowledge*. New York: Teachers College Press.

Dahlberg, G., & Moss, P. (2005). *Ethics and politics in early childhood education*. Oxfordshire, United Kingdom: RoutledgeFalmer.

Dahlberg, G., Moss, P., & Pence, A. (1999). *Beyond quality in early childhood education and care*. London: Falmer Press.

Deleuze, G., & Guattari, F. (1999). *A thousand plateaus: Capitalism and schizophrenia*. London: Athlone Press.

Fleer, M. (Ed.). (1995). *DAPcentrism: Challenging developmentally appropriate practice*. ACT: Australia Early Childhood Association.

Foucault, M. (1977). Truth and power. In C. Gordon (Ed.), *Power/knowledge: Selected interviews and other writings 1972–1977. Michel Foucault* (pp. 109–133). New York: Pantheon Books.

Foucault, M. (1980a) *Power/Knowledge: Selected interviews and other writings, 1972–1977* (C. Gordon, Ed.). London: Harvester Wheatsheaf.

Foucault, M. (1982). 'The subject and power', an afterword. In H. Dreyfus & P. Rabinow (Eds.), *Michel Foucault: Beyond structuralism and hermeneutics* (pp. 208–226). Chicago: University of Chicago Press.

Grieshaber, S., & Cannella, G. S. (Eds.). (2001). *Embracing identities in early childhood education: Diversity and possibilities.* New York: Teachers College Press.

Hatch, A., Bowman, B., Jor'dan, J. R., Morgan, C. L., Soto, L. D., Lubeck, S., et al. (2002). Developmentally appropriate practice: Continuing the dialogue. *Contemporary Issues in Early Childhood, 3*(3), 439–457.

Hughes, P., & MacNaughton, G. (1999, June). *Consensus, dissensus or community: The politics of parent involvement in early childhood education.* Paper presented at the 8th Interdisciplinary Conference on Reconceptualizing Early Childhood Education: 'Politics, Identity, & Practice', Columbus, Ohio.

Kessler, S., & Swadener, B. B. (1992). *Reconceptualizing the early childhood curriculum: Beginning the dialogue.* New York: Teachers College Press.

Keyser, (2006). *From parents to partners: Building a family-centered early childhood program.* St. Paul, MN: Redleaf Press.

Kincheloe, J. (2003). *Teachers as researchers: Qualitative inquiry as a path to empowerment* (2nd ed.). New York: Falmer.

Lubeck, S. (1998). The politics of developmentally appropriate practice: Exploring issues of culture, class, and curriculum. In B. Mallory & R. New (Eds.), *Diversity & developmentally appropriate practices: Challenges for early childhood education* (pp. 17–43). New York: Teachers College Press.

MacNaughton, G. (2003). *Shaping early childhood: Learners, curriculum and contexts.* Berkshire, England: Open University Press.

MacNaughton, G. (2005). *Doing Foucault in early childhood studies: Applying poststructural ideas.* London: Routledge.

MacNaughton, G., & Davis, K. (2001). Beyond "othering": Rethinking approaches to teaching young Anglo-Australian children about indigenous Australians. *Contemporary Issues in Early Childhood, 2*(1), 83–93.

Mallory B., & New, R. (Eds.). (1994). *Diversity & developmentally appropriate practices: Challenges for early childhood education.* New York: Teachers College Press.

Newman, B. (2005). From classrooms to the streets and back again: Real rights for refugee children. *International Journal of Equity and Innovation in Early Childhood, 3*(2), 90–93.

Reid, A. (2004). *Towards a culture of inquiry in DECS.* Government of South Australia: Department of Education and Children's Services.

Revolutionary Planning Group. (2004). Draft Manifesto. *International Journal of Equity and Innovation in Early Childhood, 2*(2), 61–62.

Robinson, K., & Jones Diaz, C. (2006). *Diversity and difference in early childhood education.* Berkshire, England: Open University Press.

Rose, N. (1999). *Powers of freedom: Reframing political thought.* Cambridge: Cambridge University Press.

Roughsey, D. (1975). *The rainbow serpent.* Sydney: HarperCollins Publishers.

Ryan, S., & Grieshaber, S. (Eds.). (2005). *Practical transformations and transformational practices: Globalization, postmodernism, and early childhood education.* Oxford, United Kingdom: Elsevier Publishing.

Sawicki, J. (1991). *Disciplining Foucault: Feminism, power, and the body.* New York: Routledge.

Weedon, C. (1997). *Feminist practice and poststructuralist theory.* Oxford, United Kingdom: Blackwell.

Yelland, N. (Ed.). (2005). *Critical issues in early childhood education.* Berkshire, England: Open University Press.

Yelland, N., & Kilderry, A. (2005). Against the tide: New ways in early childhood education. In N. Yelland (Ed.), *Critical issues in early childhood education* (pp. 1–13). Berkshire, England: Open University Press.

Mindy Blaise
Faculty of Education
Monash University

This research was supported in part by a Faculty Grant from the Faculty of Education at Monash University. The author would also like to acknowledge and thank the RPG for the minor politics they do in their everyday work with children, families, and colleagues.

Appendix A
DRAFT MANIFESTO OF THE
REVOLUTIONARY PLANNING GROUP

All revolutionary activity is a work in progress. This manifesto represents our position at this moment in time, and not for all time. The revolution is always happening.

1. INDIGENOUS CULTURE SHOULD BE CENTRAL TO ALL EARLY CHILDHOOD SERVICES

Indigenous culture should be central to all early childhood services. All services should seek to develop an ongoing relationship with their local indigenous community, and ensure that all the work of the service is informed by indigenous perspectives.

2. LEARNING SHOULD FOCUS ON CHILDREN'S STRENGTHS RATHER THAN WEAKNESSES

Deficit models of children's learning undermine children's abilities and often reinforce notions of 'difficult' children. Working from children's strengths builds positive and meaningful relationships, and helps children believe that they can learn and succeed.

3. EARLY CHILDHOOD SHOULD EMBRACE COMPLEXITY

Teaching has never been a simple task. It is not just about transmitting information, or even teaching 'values'. It is a complex, multi-faceted job, which requires a critical and reflective viewpoint.

4. LEARNING IS ONLY MEANINGFUL WHEN IT ENGAGES WITH REAL-LIFE

Teachers have a responsibility to raise local and global issues the classroom. Children can be challenged to engage with issues such as war, homelessness, global warming, consumerism, etc.

5. WE WANT TRANSFORMATION, NOT ACCEPTANCE OF THE STATUS QUO

Teaching should be acknowledged as a transformational job - we try to make a better world through education. Critical dialogue should be encouraged with children and between children, as well as across the whole early childhood community.

6. ADVOCACY FOR CHILDREN & THEIR RIGHTS IS CENTRAL TO OUR TEACHING

Children are amongst the least powerful members of society. Whenever there is a conflict between children's rights and societal practices, teachers should be courageous in speaking out.

7. EARLY CHILDHOOD IS FUNDAMENTALLY ABOUT RELATIONSHIPS

For too long early childhood has promoted the idea of the teacher as the impartial observer. This dangerous myth must be abolished. All good teaching is based on good relationships, built on trust and mutual respect.

8. CHILDREN'S IDENTITIES ARE FUNDAMENTAL TO THEIR LIVES AND THEIR LEARNING

All children navigate through a variety of cultural worlds, reflecting expectations and experiences of ethnicity, gender, class, sexuality, ability, language, etc. They are learning about power.

9. CHILDREN'S VOICES SHOULD DOMINATE THE CURRICULUM

Teaching is not about a one-way flow. Teachers should consider whose voices dominate. When do they matter, where, why, and at what cost?

10. EARLY CHILDHOOD SERVICES MUST BE OWNED BY THEIR COMMUNITY

All services should be run by and for the people who use them. Therefore all services should be not-for-profit services, run jointly by families, staff, and wherever practical, by children themselves.

JUDY WALKER

4. CREATING SPACE FOR PROFESSIONAL LEARNING

A case study of hospital play specialists

INTRODUCTION

This chapter explores the concept of professional learning in the context of a team of hospital play specialists based in a large hospital trust in the United Kingdom, University College London Hospital's NHS Foundation Trust (UCLH). This 'alternative' early childhood setting is a rich learning environment, both for supporting children's acquisition of emotionally healthy knowledge and for the development of play specialists themselves. I examine the common conflicting assumptions between hospital play specialists and other professional groups, the impact of unequal power relationships and the different discourses underpinning behavior, along with the significant progress made in resolving differences through participation and leadership in continuing professional learning. The Work Discussion Group (WDG), one of several structures created to support the development of a professional identity and continuous learning, serves as a case study for the resolution of these issues and is discussed in the final section of this chapter.

HOSPITAL PLAY SERVICES IN THE UNITED KINGDOM

Hospital-based play programs for children in the UK first emerged in the early 1960s as a result of the concerns of pediatricians for the emotional and developmental wellbeing of their patients. Admissions could be lengthy, parental visiting was limited, and opportunities for sensory stimulation and physical and cognitive development were restricted; indeed, the charity Save the Children Fund (1989) saw hospitals as a 'deprived environment for children'. The first salaried staff employed to run hospital play programs operated within the psychoanalytic tradition, where the aims were to reduce stress and possible ill effects of children's stay in hospital and promote their normal development through play. Hospital play specialists, as this new group of staff were called, were found to be crucial not only in making sure that play materials were available but to act as catalysts, without whom play might not take place. Emphasis was placed on the need for skilled observation of the way in which children play, watching for signs of stress resulting from separation from parents, and detecting the anxieties and traumas

S. Edwards, J. Nuttall (eds.), Professional Learning in Early Childhood Settings, 49–60.
© *2009 Sense Publishers. All rights reserved.*

known to accompany hospitalisation. Play designed to reduce such stress could then be introduced.

The first training for hospital play specialists was provided as a one year long day release qualification in 1976 and a standardized national qualification was introduced in 1988, progressing to a Professional Development Diploma Level 4 in 2004. Students are required to have qualifications in child care, such as the Nursery Nurse (Business & Technical Education Council) Level 3 as a prerequisite for entry. Today the focus remains on helping the child make sense of their experiences as they perceive them, their adaptation in emotionally healthy ways to the environment and to investigations and treatment, and providing them with the opportunities for satisfying and enjoyable play activities that enable development to continue to progress.

THE CHILD IN HOSPITAL

Large numbers of children experience the hospital environment each year; nearly 3 million children – 28% of the child population of England – will attend an Accident and Emergency Department, 45% will attend outpatients, and 7% will have an inpatient visit (Healthcare Commission for Healthcare Audit and Inspection, 2007). For many, these hospital attendances will be significant life events, taking place with little warning and under anxiety producing circumstances such as injury or illness. Hospitals have been largely designed with the care of adults in mind and for the adults who work in them, so that children's needs have not been accommodated. Recent building requirements for the UK National Health Service (NHS) do now specify the inclusion of baby changing facilities, separate waiting areas for children in Accident and Emergency departments and overnight accommodation for parents, and recent government investment in hospital building programs mean that more of these essentials can be provided in new hospitals from the outset.

On entering this unfamiliar environment, children are usually accompanied by a parent or caregiver who may be in a heightened state of anxiety themselves due to their concern about their child's health, and will have their own history of hospital experiences to influence their responses. If, for example, they have recently had a relative die in hospital, their grief at that loss may be triggered again. This means that the usual role taken by the adult caregiver in helping the child to make sense of their experiences may be impaired. Even when some introduction to the experience has occurred through previous visits, a family member's experiences, school based learning or pre-admission education programs, each hospital attendance will challenge the child with new social encounters, novel physical sensations, new sights, and new opportunities for learning.

The child will arrive in hospital having already acquired some information from a variety of sources, such as television or friends' accounts, about what a hospital experience might involve, but may not have actively engaged with that information or had the support of someone else to transform it into something meaningful. The child also arrives with a particular set of culturally-specific values about how to behave in the hospital environment and how staff may behave towards the child and family, along with parallel knowledge about what to do when ill or injured. For example, a French mother was disappointed because the doctor only wrote a prescription for one medicine for her child; in France she would expect to always have at least three items prescribed. In another example, it is only recently in the UK that the cultural concept of children wearing everyday clothes rather than pyjamas while in hospital has become the norm on children's wards, although it is still common on adult wards. If there is no such information available to the child in their regular cultural setting, it may be borrowed from rules applied in other settings, such as schools. Many children of school age sit quietly by their beds, having learnt that permission is required to play in official settings, even when play equipment is visible and close to the hospital bed. Pre-school children, by contrast, will move freely around the ward or clinic, unless limited by their parents.

The hospital play specialist is a mediator for the child and her or his experiences in the hospital environment, using play to take children beyond their everyday understandings to form new meanings and knowledge. This learning may include concepts about the hospital staff who care for them, the causation of illness, and the purpose of treatments. For example, children with cancer who require radiotherapy treatment will frequently be told that it is 'sunshine treatment' involving 'rays'. These explanations do not supply enough detail and can be the cause of misconceptions; many children know that sunshine and 'rays' can burn and hurt skin. The hospital play specialist will enable children to explore these ideas and engage with the environment, materials, and machines in a way which allows them to construct their own realistic ideas and master their fears. For example, a five-year-old child in clinic was reported to be refusing to eat. He had suffered a large cut to his knee that became infected and it was through play that the hospital play specialist identified the reasons behind his food refusal. Having seen fluid and scabs coming away from his knee, he became concerned that the food he ate would come out of the hole in his knee.

Each social interaction in the hospital will provide opportunities for the child patient to build on her or his knowledge but the play specialist has the particular task of facilitating the transformation of learning. And it is the observations made of the child and the information gathered from his or her caregivers that will form the basis of the planning and interventions undertaken rather than starting from traditional developmental norms.

THE WORK AND LEARNING CONTEXT FOR HOSPITAL PLAY SPECIALISTS

Cheek and Rudge (1994) examined the hospital case notes of adult patients through a postmodern variant of discourse analysis and found that the personal experience and knowledge of the patients was notably absent from the case notes, which were almost exclusively dominated by the rational scientific voice of medicine: blood results, urine outputs, fluid balances. Medical and, to some extent, nursing staff construct their reality of the patient from a very different perspective to that of hospital play specialists. Furthermore, medicine has until recently been a largely male-dominated profession and this has meant that the hierarchy of hospitals has been dominated by a masculine cultural code of detached autonomy, control, and mastery of others. Ninety-eight percent of hospital play specialists are female and their cultural code places value on selflessness, relatedness, understanding, and group orientation, which give a different perspective on the way they see the world and act within it (Davies, 1995).

These and many other differences in discourses and cultural codes have meant there have been particular challenges for hospital play specialists to explore in over four decades of work in hospital as they interact with multi-professional groups on a daily basis. Hospital play specialists are unique amongst early childhood educators in engaging in these multiple overlapping activity systems and have been doing this while still developing professional identities in an ever-changing health service environment. Working alongside medical and nursing colleagues, with their long established professional roles and clear hierarchies, play specialists are at risk from feeling and being undervalued, isolated, and frustrated in their jobs. With the word "play" in their job title, and dealing with assumptions about the low significance of playful activity in an environment committed to heroic attempts to save lives, staff frequently experience difficulties in their interactions with other staff.

The example of vene-puncture intervention serves to illustrate these difficulties. There is good research evidence to demonstrate the benefits of distraction activities to significantly reduce children's distress and pain during vene-puncture and other invasive procedures (Uman, et al., 2006). To be able to carry out these anxiety-reducing techniques, the play specialist needs to be called by doctors or nurses *before* the procedure is begun. However this is frequently not done and this is a recurring issue in most hospital play specialists' working lives. For medical and nursing staff, blood tests are routine in nature and often perceived as 'just a little scratch'. Their knowledge centres on the skills of locating and accessing veins, extracting the volume of blood required and the number of specimen bottles needed, rather than the emotional impact of the procedure on the child. This means awareness of the need for a play specialist to lead distraction play and to coach and praise the child may be limited, and the play specialist is called only when the child's behaviour becomes unmanageable. Recurring difficulties of this type are experienced by play specialists in their interactions with medical staff due to the differences in assumptions between each group of staff and the unequal balance of the power between them.

Working alongside medical and nursing staff who do not understand and value their work can be demoralising and de-motivating for hospital play specialists, especially if there is active resistance or obstruction to their work. No early childhood educator would need to justify the value of messy play for young children but resistance to such play is frequently encountered in hospital with clinical safety cited as a (spurious) justification. To be effective in advocacy for children and in supporting children's learning, play specialists have to be confident in their goals and functions within the multi-professional team and be able to counter resistance with professional integrity.

Engaging in multi-site teams, either on separate wards or across hospital departments located in different buildings, provides a further challenge in ensuring high standards in the provision of play services. When an individual's work is visible to others who are knowledgeable about it, and where it is open to discussion and reflection and evaluation, practice is more likely to grow and develop in quality, but shared locations are not usually the case for hospital play specialists.

THE CHANGING WORK CONTEXT FOR HOSPITAL PLAY SPECIALISTS AT UCLH

In a relatively short period of time the numbers of hospital play specialists employed at UCLH grew from six (in 2003) to 16 (in 2007). This increase in numbers was not mirrored elsewhere in the UK. Expansion in the size of the hospital play team was not deliberately planned but arose in response to two significant forces that highlighted the non-medical needs of children in hospital. One of these was the report of the Bristol Royal Infirmary Public Inquiry (The Kennedy Report, 2002), which uncovered the grim reality that more that thirty infants and children who had cardiac surgery over a four year period needlessly died due to the incompetence of an individual surgeon. The report revealed that children were still largely being treated as 'small adults' in the medical, organisational, and managerial structures of hospitals, and that family-centred care fell far short of expected standards. A *National Service Framework for Children and Young People* (Department of Health, Department for Education and Skills 14 September 2004) was published to give clear guidance and this has been followed up by annual audits by the Healthcare Commission of the extent to which hospitals are meeting the Framework standards. This was a significant cultural shift, forcing UCLH and hospitals across the UK to put children's issues further up the agenda than they might previously have done.

The second factor contributing to the growth of the play service at UCLH, and the increase in understanding of its value, was the participation by the small team of hospital play specialists in multi-professional clinical team meetings within the hospital and my leadership in the role of Play Services Manager. By engaging with the institutional landscape, using the artefacts and language that it provides, and by bringing our work to the attention of others, the way was prepared for a mutual transformation of understanding. When external charitable funding was secured in 1999 for a hospital play specialist in the radiotherapy department, we had been providing occasional support for highly distressed children for some months and it was clear to me that a play specialist based in the department was needed. However the Technological Services Departmental Manager was openly averse to the employment of a (charity funded) play specialist post, stating that she saw no need for the role. After one year, the same manager apologised for her lack of understanding and was fully supportive of the participation of the play specialist in the care of children in her department, having witnessed for herself the 'work' of play and engaging in frequent dialogue with the hospital play specialist. Similar transformations have happened in each department where hospital play services have been introduced. The play specialists themselves have led this transformation, but it has needed leadership to pave the way and provide support for staff in hostile environments.

THE PROFESSIONAL LEARNING NEEDS OF HOSPITAL PLAY SPECIALISTS

The role of hospital play specialists requires that they work with children and their families during some very distressing experiences. In contrast to the medical staff's need for clinical detachment, play specialists need to engage with the child's emotional journey if the therapist is to support the child's learning and emotional health. Even a child admitted for a straightforward day case admission for dental surgery will be experiencing high anxiety. At UCLH the surgical play specialist's task is to use play to introduce key concepts to the child in the short time available before the therapist accompanies her or him to the anaesthetic room. Attention will be paid to the child's understanding of events, and questioning and coping behaviours are encouraged. Games and playful activity to manage anxiety are used on the journey to the operating room, while acknowledging any concerns expressed. If the child becomes distressed, the play specialist will support the parent in helping their child or intervene if appropriate, using coaching and distraction strategies as required. Once the child is sedated, the parent's distress is responded to sympathetically on the return journey to the ward and during the waiting period. The play specialist may implement this procedure for six children each morning, five mornings a week.

The concept of burnout has frequently been studied in the nursing profession but not in hospital play. However, experience has demonstrated to me that it does occur and, if one studies the variables which contribute to it, it would be surprising not to have play staff feeling stressed and approaching burnout. Omdahl and O'Donnell (1999) describe the results of burnout as depersonalisation, reduced personal accomplishment, emotional exhaustion, and reduced occupational commitment. Their research illustrates how the caring, empathetic aspect of nursing work can contribute both to burnout and to greater job satisfaction. Three empathy variables were described and examined in 164 nurses in two United States hospitals: emotional contagion (sharing, taking on the emotion of another person); empathetic concern (concern for the well being of another); and communicative responsiveness (effectively communicate with others about sensitive and emotional topics). A clear pattern emerged in the findings, whereby emotional contagion was positively associated with burnout, while emotional concern and communicative responsiveness were negatively associated with burnout. In other words, if professionals identify with or take on the emotion of others, they are more likely to become emotionally exhausted and leave the nursing profession. But the more the nurses were able to communicate effectively with their patients, the *less* depersonalisation they experienced. Also, the more they were able to recognise and show concern for patients' emotional needs the more job satisfaction they felt.

Hospital play specialists are particularly vulnerable to emotional contagion, with all-day involvement with children and their families, sometimes over many weeks and months, without the protection of a uniform and task-orientated schedules afforded to professions such as nursing. To do their job well, play specialists have to be able to see the hospital experience from the child's perspective. This makes it imperative for play staff to be able to know when they are experiencing empathic concern, and to identify and use strategies to promote empathic concern whilst avoiding emotional contagion and burnout.

To summarise, the professional learning challenges facing this group of staff include geographical organisation from one another across the multiple wards and sites of the hospital, a highly medicalised model of care that devalues child focused play based activity and learning, and the vulnerability of professional boundaries due to the highly empathetic nature of the hospital play specialists' work. These conditions frame the possibilities for professional learning available to the team.

CREATING SPACE FOR PROFESSIONAL LEARNING

Although staff employed as hospital play specialists at UCLH hold the BTEC Professional Development Diploma in Specialised Play for the Sick Child, a national qualification which prepares them well for the role, there are no further profession-specific qualifications available. With limited opportunities for career progression existing in a small profession, and a high level of "mature" entrants from other allied roles, play specialists tend to stay in post for long periods. The responsibility to ensure there are continuing professional development opportunities throughout the play specialists' employment rests with play therapy managers such as myself, and is recognised within the clinical governance structures of the UCLH as an important risk management activity.

As the team grew in numbers, in the way described earlier in this chapter, my clinical work on the wards reduced and the way I led the staff had to change. Absorbing new staff into the group and enabling them to participate in the cultural activities of the group became an essential goal. With most staff working as sole practitioners in different wards, sometimes in different buildings, the need to build their identity as part of a professional group was paramount.

Since my leadership of the play team grew alongside my own work as a play specialist, a traditional hierarchical pattern would not have been possible, despite it being the dominant model in the hospital. Instead, I found myself developing an approach more akin to a 'post-modern' definition of leadership: visionary, empowering, flat, decentralised, and people centred. Initially, this took the form of shared storytelling and learning together, as I described my own work with children and families to my team, sharing insights and reflections on my and their interactions with patients and staff. Such dialogue happened without formal structures, due to the proximity of our workplaces, and I carried out few of the management formalities common in the other professional groupings, such as competency workbooks, formal appraisal, or activity planning. Perhaps because I was the only play specialist during my initial years at UCLH and experienced no direct line management, my model of leadership viewed individuals' experience as the starting point for learning, as it had been for me, rather than adopting a task-orientated, top-down style.

It is important to remember that the work being undertaken at UCLH to support professional learning is happening in the wider context of an emergent profession, which is still in the process of developing its own identity, clarifying the purposes of its activity, and defining its common assumptions. This means there are few reference points for professional learning strategies available within the profession itself so the structures used by other disciplines have been used as inspirations for our own. The closest parallels available in the hospital are the Child and Adolescent Mental Health Service (CAMHS), composed of child psychotherapists, psychologists, and psychiatrists, who have clinical supervision at the heart of their approach to professional learning. In the final section of this chapter I describe how the team of hospital play specialists at UCLH has adopted aspects of the CAMHS clinical supervision model to learn from the particular challenges faced when providing play services in the medical environment. I describe the concepts and structures that have developed to promote professional learning in the team, and how these have stemmed directly from our work with children, families, and colleagues.

THE WORK DISCUSSION GROUP

The Work Discussion Group (WDG) is central to professional learning for hospital play specialists at UCLH. Meeting for an hour per week every week of the year, there is a continuing rota so that members of the team know several weeks in advance when they are due to make a presentation to the WDG. When it is their turn, the play specialist brings a typed observation of an element of their work with copies for each member of the group. Written out with an introduction to the child's diagnosis, family members, and a brief medical history, the play specialist will initially read the text aloud. Some participants take notes as they listen and questions may be asked at this stage to clarify factual information.

The play specialist's observation may be of a single play session, an episode or a conversation, or report interactions with a patient over some days or weeks. Detail about the child's verbal and non-verbal communication is included and the play specialists' accounts include reflections about how they felt at the time, and what they did or said in response. Interpretations of the child's behaviour or dialogue are not encouraged in the written observation. No guidance is given on the length of the presentation but a standard length of approximately 1000 words has emerged and the presentation usually occupies the first 15 to 20 minutes of the meeting. A group discussion follows, which may include further questioning about the medical condition of the child, the interactions and feelings involved, comments about similarities with other situations, descriptions of personal and professional reactions to the material presented, and ideas about what the play specialist could do in future interactions with the same or similar patients.

The group is co-facilitated by me and a child psychotherapist who has worked closely with play specialists for many years. She comes with a great respect for the contribution of play specialists to the emotional health of hospitalised children and an appreciation of the immediacy of our engagement with children. This dual leadership of the group enables different roles to be fulfilled and echoes the traditional family of two adult 'parents'. Some staff members respond positively to this conceptualisation, appreciating the sense of safety a supportive parent can bring. Others have times when they wish to challenge it; for example, by steering discussion outside the usual format or by requesting that the WDG be replaced with monthly staff meetings.

There is a high level of voluntary attendance and only long term students are invited to attend, to maintain the cohesion of the group. The observations brought for discussion may include successful outcomes to interventions as well as ongoing work with very sick patients and work where the outcome was not 'successful'. Interactions with other professionals and family members may be included but will not be the main focus. The play specialists bring their observations for different reasons; as one reflected, "The cases choose themselves".

Initial responses from colleagues to the presentation are often reassurance and validation for the feelings shown and responses in the situation described. This reflects the often painful feelings voiced or shown by the presenter and the group members may desire to make everything alright. Hawkins and Shohet (2000), in writing about supervision in the helping professions, say that "the supervisor's role is not just to reassure the worker but to allow the emotional disturbance to be felt within the safer setting of the supervisory relationship, where it can be survived, reflected upon and learned from. Supervision thus provides a container that holds the helping relationship within the therapeutic triad" (p. 3) This triad in our group consists of the patient (and family), the collective hospital play specialist role as well as the individual presenter, and the Group facilitators. The role of the psychotherapist is to contain disturbing feelings so that they can be acknowledged and explored. This is what Proctor (1988) calls the 'restorative' function of supervision, where supervisees allow "themselves to be affected by the distress, pain and fragmentation of the client [in our case the child patient] and to become aware of how this has affected them and to deal with any reactions" (p. 50). For example, one play specialist made a case presentation describing how she had taken the lead when a child stopped breathing; although the presentation occurred several weeks after the emergency had taken place, the structure of the WDG provided her with the space to revisit feelings she had not had time, or felt able, to process before.

Proctor (1988) describes a second function of supervision as 'formative'. This aspect is about developing the skills, understanding, and abilities of the supervisees to look at how they intervened and the consequences of their interventions. In a gentle way, our everyday understandings of the interaction with the patient, family or colleagues is examined and assumptions challenged, so that further insights are gained. One of the hardest things for staff to bear is to not know with any certainty what might be being experienced by the child and whether their intervention has made a positive contribution to the child's learning. To fill this 'not knowing' void, concepts from our own childhood experiences, our own family traditions, or medical and nursing perspectives may be used. Hawkins and Shohet (2000) write that "supervision can give us the chance to stand back and reflect; a chance to avoid the easy way out of blaming others – clients, peers, the organisation, society or even oneself; and it can give us a chance to engage in the search for new options, to discover the learning that often emerges from the most difficult situations and to get support" (p. 3). Postmodernism accepts that there are many different ways of looking at the world and that there is no single set of standards by which to judge which of these ways is better than the others. Our Work Discussion Group enables us to put a 'pause' button on our responses to the contrasting cultural norms of the medical and nursing staff or the organisational structures of the hospital that may cause problems for our patients. This allows the team to become open to other, less 'black and white', responses and reclaim the particular task that belongs to the hospital play specialist.

The third function of supervision described by Proctor (1988) is 'normative' and provides a 'quality control' function for work with people. Johns (2000) argues that individual prejudices also contribute to the need for professional staff to reflect on their work practices. The Work Discussion Group is not a managerial structure but there are occasions when managerial actions arise as a result of the discussions. For example, one staff member's encounter with a violent post-operative seven-year-old patient led to a multi-professional review of the patient pathways for children with diagnosed behaviour problems.

The structure of the Work Discussion Group is determined by the turn-taking nature of the rota, the written format of each case, the careful preparation done prior to the meeting in the writing up of the observation, and the predictable flow of the one-hour meetings. These structuring devices have a containing effect for the group whilst allowing knowledge to be developed by the group and individuals. The choice of subject matter allows something to be recognised as a problem for the self as well as by others in the group. As a manager, I could define the 'problems' that need 'fixing' and come up with 'solutions', but this independent identification of problems in the WDG has the benefit of being directly relevant to the individual play specialist and their own personal and clinical context. My purpose is to ensure that staff competencies, and the skills and knowledge that underpin them, are relevant and responsive to the complex situations in which staff work.

THE WORK DISCUSSION GROUP AS A SITE FOR PROFESSIONAL LEARNING

Having chosen the 'work' to be brought to the group, the play specialist begins her own learning by reviewing the experience as it is written down. It continues when she reads what she has written aloud to the Group and hears for herself what she experienced. The responses of her peer group give further perspectives on these experiences. Some of these responses may be emotional or immature, and one of the roles of the co-facilitators is to remind members of the Group of the limits of our knowledge and the scope of our professional practice, as well giving a wider perspective and making links to previously discussed themes. I am somewhat uncomfortable with the term 'leadership' to describe my role here, as we are all learning together, but I and the child psychotherapist do need to guide the group's learning so that mature responses to challenging situations can be constructed. One recurring theme in presentations is the sense of loss or helplessness when a child dies or leaves the hospital in less than ideal circumstances, such as being taken to an emergency foster home. The desire to blame others for perceived failings and identification with the child or parent in these circumstances can be strong, and feelings need to be named and acknowledged by the leaders to facilitate a constructive response rather than a destructive one.

Our experience is that the witnessing of our experiences and observations to and by each other legitimises the professional work of hospital play specialists, and allows knowledge to be socially constructed as well experienced personally. Also, the weekly nature of the group addresses some of the isolation issues caused by the geographical environment in which our play services are provided, by bringing together the whole team. Meeting together has a cohesive effect in itself but it is the sharing of our work that confirms what it is we do and why. This does the most to support our learning and the construction of our professional identities.

The concepts and structure underpinning the WDG also mirror for staff some of the features of our work with children. Play specialists come from a range of social and cultural backgrounds and work in very diverse clinical settings, including the Emergency Department, a children's cancer ward, and a dental hospital, so have different learning needs which change during their employment. Being given space to explore and reflect and to have their own perspective acknowledged mirrors the approach taken with our young patients. The term 'learning community' applies to the spirit as much as the reality of our situation. This learning community is self-sustaining and does not require financial resources, other than the one hour per week contributed by a skilled child psychotherapist. Nor is administrative authorisation required and this adds to its strength. Having started with no assumptions about what 'ought' to be provided and no material resources, we have been free to create our own structures.

CONCLUSION

Leading the development of a service with few external constraints has allowed me to focus on what our child patients need, what the hospital play specialists need to learn to meet children's needs, and how I can best provide for those needs as a leader and manager. One of the features of professional learning at UCLH is that much of it takes place within and from the workplace itself. Staff do attend external courses and conferences but, as I noted earlier, there is little available that is profession-specific within the UK. These circumstances have intensified both the need for, and the benefits of, hospital-based professional learning structures. Therapists are learning from their own work and make connections, based on their own reflections, which are relevant to their own settings. The outcomes of this process mirror the components found by Louis, Marks, and Kruse (1996) to be significant in schools as learning communities, especially the shared sense of purpose, the collective focus on child learning, de-privatised activity, and reflective dialogues.

I have been in the privileged position of creating a play department from scratch, resulting in a group culture where staff can support children's learning and adaptation in hospital in a way that reaches beyond the taken-for-granted aspects of play activities to a therapeutic conceptualisation of the child's experience. There has, as yet, been no formal evaluation of the Work Discussion Group and the other structures which have been created to contribute to professional learning. However, there has been a noticeable difference in the professional standing of hospital play specialists within UCLH, demonstrated in the growth in demand for their services across many clinical areas and the intolerance shown by local clinical staff to play specialists being unavailable due to sick leave. I believe this is due to the quality of the work each of them undertakes with children and the confidence with which they are able to interact with all levels in multi-professional teams, which I would argue is sustained by the continuing professional learning in which they engage.

REFERENCES

Cheek, J., & Rudge, T. (1994). Inquiry into nursing as textually mediated discourse. In P. Chinn (Ed.), *Advances in methods of inquiry for nursing* (pp. 213–215). Gaithersburg, MD: Aspen.

Davies, C. (1995). *Gender and the professional predicament in nursing.* Buckingham: Open University Press.

Department of Health, Department for Education and Skills. (2004, September 14). *A national service framework for children and young people.* London: The Stationary Office Crown Publications.

Hawkins, P., & Shohet, R. (2000). *Supervising in the helping professions: An individual group and organisational approach* (2nd ed.). Milton Keynes: Open University Press.

Healthcare Commission for Healthcare Audit and Inspection. (2007). *Improving services for children in hospital.* London.

Johns, C. (2000). *Constructing a philosophy for practice: Becoming a reflective practitioner.* Oxford: Blackwell Press.

Kennedy, I. (2001). *Learning from Bristol: The report of the public inquiry into children's heart surgery at the Bristol Royal Infirmary 1984–1995* [The Kennedy Report]. London: Crown Publications.

Louis, K. S., Marks, H., & Kruse, S. (1996). Teachers' professional communities in restructuring schools. *American Educational Research Journal, 33*(4), 757–798.

Omdahl, B. L., & O'Donnell, C. (1999). Emotional contagion, empathetic concern and communicative responsiveness as variables affecting nurses' stress and occupational commitment. *Journal of Advanced Nursing, 29*(6), 1351–1359.

Proctor, B. (1988). Supervision: A co-operative exercise in accountability. In M. Marken & M. Payne (Eds.), *Enabling and ensuring* (pp. 21–23). Leicester: National Youth Bureau and Council for Education and Training in Youth and Community Work.

Save the Children Fund. (1989). *A deprived environment for children: The case for hospital play schemes.* London: Save the Children Fund.

Uman, L. S., Chambers, C. T., McGrath, P. J., & Kisely, S. (2008). Psychological interventions for needle-related procedural pain and distress in children and adolescents. [Systematic Review] *Cochrane Database of Systematic Reviews, 3.* Retrieved October 28, 2008, from http://ovidsp.tx.ovid.com.ezproxy.lib.monash.edu.au/spb/ovidweb

Judy Walker
University College London Hospitals NHS Foundation Trust

CARMEN DALLI AND SUE CHERRINGTON

5. ETHICAL PRACTICE AS RELATIONAL WORK

A New Frontier for Professional Learning?

INTRODUCTION

As in many other Western countries, change has been the hallmark of the New Zealand early childhood scene over the last two decades. Change has occurred at the level of administrative structures, at the level of policy, and at the level of pedagogy. Along the way, the New Zealand early childhood sector has been transformed from one divided along historical, philosophical, administrative, and funding lines to one that is united around a common curriculum framework[1], a shared funding structure and a coherent policy framework[2] (Ministry of Education, 2002) that aims to ensure that by 2012 all teacher-led early childhood services will be staffed by qualified teachers.

TOWARDS A CODE OF ETHICS

The events and dynamics that have produced this transformation have been chronicled elsewhere (e.g., Dalli, 2003a; Dalli & Te One, 2004; May, 2007; Meade, 1990). Part of this chapter adds to that story: We recount how at a time of policy retrenchment and an adverse public profile for the sector, the advocacy actions of a group of tertiary academics, union activists and early childhood practitioners, succeeded in mobilising a sector-wide initiative around the development of the New Zealand Early Childhood Code of Ethics that created a counter-discourse to the negative one that prevailed at that time. We argue that this work contributed to the transformation of the sector. It created a groundswell for a discourse of professionalism; it led to the introduction of a focus on professional ethics within teacher preparation programmes across the country; and it has contributed to the growth of a culture of professional reflection within the sector.

Both of us were members of the national working group that between 1993 and 1995 engaged in a national consultation process that produced the NZ Early Childhood Code of Ethics. Within that project we were responsible for the national survey conducted at the start of the process. The survey gathered data on the types of situations of ethical difficulty that early childhood educators faced in their daily practice (Dalli & Cherrington, 1994). Ten years later, we conducted a follow-up of that original survey with the aim of investigating the 'life' of the Code of Ethics in the daily practice of contemporary early childhood teachers. As in the original survey, we asked qualified early childhood educators to identify situations of

S. Edwards, J. Nuttall (eds.), Professional Learning in Early Childhood Settings, 61–80.

ethical difficulty in their practice and to describe their response to them. The follow-up survey, conducted over the final months of 2003 and early 2004, also asked teachers to nominate qualities needed to be "professional" and how they would recognize early childhood professionalism in interactions with children, colleagues, parents and other family members, management, outside agencies and in wider community settings (see Dalli, 2006a).

Against the background of this story, in the rest of this chapter we draw on our joint work on these two national surveys to respond to the task of this book: to articulate new ways of thinking about professional learning in a post-developmental era. We draw on the surveys in two ways: Firstly we argue that the surveys illustrate that early childhood work is complex, frequently troubling and inevitably ethical. Secondly, we argue that at a time of heightened interest in what it means to be professional in early childhood education, it is timely to foreground the complexity of early childhood work and take on the challenge of re-visioning professional practice as ethical practice, and professional learning as ethically grounded. We conclude with an exploration of what this might mean in the changing world of early childhood.

ADVOCACY FOR A CODE OF ETHICS[3]: CREATING A DISCOURSE OF PROFESSIONALISM

The early 1990s was a time of policy retrenchment and low morale for the sector (see Dalli, 1993). During the late 1980s, a restructuring of all aspects of state responsibility had resulted in a massive change in Education. For the early childhood sector this led to the first comprehensive review of the sector, the Meade Report (Meade, 1988) and the subsequent Before Five policies (Lange, 1988). The Before Five policies addressed themselves to resolving long-standing issues within the sector including issues of equity of access, equity of funding, measures to ensure quality, and ways of redressing the low status of early childhood work. The policies created much optimism in the sector which was, however, to be short-lived. A change of government in November 1990 was accompanied by the dismantling of the Before Five policies and the beginning of a period of policy retrenchment (Dalli, 1993; Dalli, 2003a; Meade & Dalli, 1991; May, 2001; Meade, 1995; Mitchell, 1995; Wells, 1999).

Alongside the dismantling of the Before Five policies, in the early 1990s the early childhood sector was the focus of much unfavourable media attention through a spate of reports of allegations of child abuse in centres. The professional embarrassment of such allegations for early childhood practitioners was intense and caused considerable distress in the sector (Duncan, 1998).

Within this context, when, in early 1993, the New Zealand Council for Educational Research (NZCER) organised a national seminar on the role of government in early childhood education, the mood of the conference was not a happy one. The address by the then Minister of Education, the Hon Lockwood Smith, confirmed that Government saw its role in early childhood education as largely a hands-off one. It was also clear that the Minister saw the sector as too diverse to act effectively as a coherent lobby group (Smith, 1993). One of us (Dalli) was present at the conference and, in discussing the general despondency of the sector with Linda Mitchell, a strong unionist and early childhood advocate, a plan started to take shape to develop an early childhood Code of Ethics using well-tested strategies of advocacy (e.g., Robinson & Stark, 2002): getting organized; creating a proactive agenda; developing the message; and working with others. Our proactive agenda was to counter the despondency of the sector and rally early childhood people around a positive initiative that would give the public a message about the sector's commitment to high standards of professional practice.

The first step in 'getting organized' was to contact other people who had an interest in professional practice and to form a national working group. The early childhood union of the time, CECUA (the Combined Early Childhood Union of Aotearoa) immediately offered secretarial and office support. Two other early childhood organisations, FECEO (Federation of Early Childhood Education Organisations[4]), and OMEP-Aotearoa New Zealand (Organisation Mondiale pour l'Education Préscolaire), offered to act as the umbrella organisations for the project. Following the first meeting of the working group, an advisory committee was formed that represented the broad range of early childhood organisations and services and shortly afterwards, a research grant from Victoria University of Wellington[5] to one of us (Dalli) enabled the project to embark on a major data gathering activity: a national survey of qualified early childhood educators in 600 randomly selected early childhood centres. The aim of the survey was to identify areas of professional work that created situations of ethical difficulties and to understand the ways in which practitioners responded to these situations.

From here the process snowballed into a kind of action research project that involved practitioners at each step of the planning, acting and evaluating cycle. Alongside the work on the survey, two sets of workshop materials were devised with financial support from the New Zealand Teacher Registration Board. The materials were packaged as Education Kits and included a video which explained the process of the development of the Code of Ethics, and presented selected scenarios of ethical situations reported by early childhood educators in the national survey. Practitioners were asked to work through these scenarios and send feedback to the national working group about how they would respond in those situations. These data, together with the analysis of the survey data, enabled the working group to identify sixty values that appeared to underlie early childhood practitioners' professional responses to the scenarios. Further analysis enabled the working group to organize the sixty values around six categories that were formulated as a draft Code of Ethics. A Ministry of Education grant then enabled the draft code to be sent, via an Early Childhood Development Unit[6] (ECDU) mail-out, to all licensed, chartered early childhood services for comment. The feedback from this process informed the final Code of Ethics in which the values were worded in terms of what early childhood educators valued as the rights of children; parents/whanau[7]/ caregivers; tangata whenua[8]; community and society; self and colleagues; and employment.

Within this developmental process, both the survey and the educational kits were planned as consultative, information sharing mechanisms through which discussion could be generated about professional ethical issues faced by the early childhood community. Additionally, throughout the project, the national working group received numerous invitations to present workshops and seminars about the Code and this led to the production of a set of resources to accompany the Code that could be used for professional development purposes. This was in line with the objective of the national working group that the process of developing the code would be a developmental one for the sector (Dalli & Mitchell, 1995). The resources produced include a booklet that clarifies how the Code of Ethics relates to early childhood educators' legal obligations and how the Code may be of use in daily practice. At the time of writing, there have been multiple reprints of these resources which continue to be used by teacher education institutions nationwide.

That the objective of broad consultation and engagement in professional development was achieved was noted at the launch of the Code of Ethics in 1995. Speaking on behalf of the national working group, Dalli and Mitchell (1995) noted:

This code of ethics is based on widespread consultation throughout all services. We can take strength from the many hundreds of early childhood educators who have helped in its development and know that we have the backing of the early childhood profession when we use the code of ethics in our advocacy (p. 73).

Referring to the climate of suspicion that hung around early childhood centres in the early 1990s, Dalli and Mitchell (1995) added that the national working group:

... felt that a Code of Ethics would not only provide protection for children and staff but it would also be a means for the early childhood sector to assert its professional values: It was one way the sector could show [that] it stood for far more than the media publicity was projecting (p. 69).

Dalli and Mitchell continued:

Another major reason for developing this Code is related to promoting the status of early childhood work as a profession. Having a code of ethics is often seen as one of the clearest indications of professionalism (p. 69).

From the start then, the Code of Ethics project was simultaneously an act of professional development as well as an attempt to create a counter-movement, or a counter discourse to the dominant hostile policy environment. Additionally, it was consciously and deliberately an attempt to claim the ground of professional status for the early childhood education sector. It was an attempt to challenge the *status quo* and transform the professional *habitus* (Cunningham, 1993; Bourdieu & Passeron, 1971). Thus it was also a political act of self-determination that laid the foundation for an emerging discourse of professionalism that was to gather momentum in the new millennium (e.g., Dalli, 2003b).

At the launch of the Code at the Early Childhood Convention in 1995, the national working group declared itself disbanded and the Code was handed over to

FECEO and OMEP Aotearoa/New Zealand with responsibility for guiding the Code forward in the life of the sector. In the absence of a single professional body for all early childhood practitioners, the process of formal acceptance of the Code was left to individual early childhood organisations to manage. NZEI Te Riu Roa[9], which was the union of the majority of early childhood staff, adopted the Code unanimously at its annual general meeting in September 1996, alongside other early childhood organizations. In all cases, the Code was seen as an aspirational document; no organization put in processes to monitor its use.

In the first few years after the launch of the Code, members of the National Working Group were often invited to run workshops about how the Code could be a tool for professional learning and practice. Currently, this work is mostly done by lecturers in pre-service and in-service teacher education courses offered by universities and other training providers. Requests for copies of the Code and accompanying materials continue to be made to the main teachers' union, NZEI, which now looks after re-printing the materials. However, until the second national survey (referred to earlier in this chapter) was carried out in 2003, no systematic research on the impact of the Code of Ethics had been undertaken.

The second survey was conducted in the context of a heightened discourse of early childhood professionalism (Dalli, 2003b). We were also aware that the recently established New Zealand Teachers' Council (NZTC) was required, by legislation, to develop a binding code for all registered teachers. As the NZTC began this work, early public statements referred to the Early Childhood Code of Ethics as a good model for other parts of the education system. It therefore seemed timely to gather systematic data on how early childhood practitioners viewed and worked with the Early Childhood code of ethics before a more general Code of Ethics was formulated.

EARLY CHILDHOOD WORK AS COMPLEX, TROUBLING AND INEVITABLY ETHICAL: NEW WAYS OF THINKING ABOUT PROFESSIONAL PRACTICE

The data from our two surveys provide clear evidence that early childhood work is complex, frequently troubling and often raises ethical issues. Both surveys were conducted by postal questionnaire sent to approximately 600 randomly selected licensed early childhood centres with a request that the respondent be a qualified practitioner. This request was premised on the assumption that qualified practitioners could be expected to have a heightened awareness of ethical aspects of their work; since one of the objectives of the surveys was to elicit actual examples of ethical dilemmas that early childhood practitioners met in their day-to-day practice, it was important that respondents recognized ethical issues when these arose. Additionally, our request reflected our political agenda of claiming the ground of professional status for the early childhood sector: Although ethical practice may not be the prerogative of qualified staff, by requesting responses from qualified practitioners, we deliberately positioned qualifications as a valued component of the professional role.

In our work in developing the Code of Ethics, the National Working Group had adopted the definition of an ethical dilemma articulated by Kipnis (1987), an American philosopher who had been a key player in the development of the NAEYC Code of Ethics. According to Kipnis, an ethical dilemma arises "when two or more core [professional] values are in conflict" (p. 28). By contrast, a "difficult situation" may be unpleasant or hard to resolve but it does not involve the same level of conflict between core professional values (Newman, 1998).

In both surveys, early childhood educators reported a great number of situations that they identified as posing ethical difficulties: In the 1994 survey we asked two questions intended to elicit examples of such situations. In answer, the 322 (53.5% return rate) respondents described a total of 1716 situations with each respondent describing an average of five ethically troubling situations. In the 2004 survey, only one question was posed to gather such examples. In this later survey, the average number of situations reported by each respondent was two, with the total number of respondents (n=262; 44% return rate) describing 529 situations between them.

In this section we explore what these situations reveal about the complex and troubling nature of early childhood teaching. While many of these situations may qualify more as 'difficult situations' (Newman, 1998) than as "ethical dilemmas" (Kipnis, 1987), they nonetheless illustrate situations in which ethical issues are implicated. We argue that the ethics involved in responding to these practice situations are not solely based on notions of rights but rather reflect the particular context of early childhood work. This context is attentive to relationships and imbued with notions of care and a sense of responsibility for the well-being of children and their families. Moreover, we invite readers to think about the implications for professional learning inherent in each of these cases, and to make links between their own professional learning and their experience of difficult situations and ethical dilemmas.

EARLY CHILDHOOD WORK AS COMPLEX AND TROUBLING

A key aspect of early childhood work is that it requires the practitioner to interact with a wide range of people: children, the adults that look after the children, colleagues within the same early childhood setting and beyond, centre management, the wider community, and officials from a host of outside agencies. In New Zealand outside agencies include the Ministry of Education, Work and Income New Zealand, and the Child, Youth and Family Service.

This array of different people is a primary contributor to the complexity of the early childhood practitioner's role (Feeney & Freeman, 1999). Our surveys showed that, even when an early childhood teacher's work was mainly focused on daily interactions with children, the other work-related relationships in which teachers participated created numerous complex intersections with their relationships with children and were often the source of conflicting demands and ethically difficult situations. Through analysing the relationship dimensions within which the difficult situations unfolded, it is possible to render visible the highly contextualised nature of early childhood teaching and to infer the continuing professional learning that occurs in these contexts.

Example 1: Dealing with separated parents

Situations involving custody issues featured prominently among the most challenging, and sometimes distressing, challenges for teachers. The respondents reported feeling like 'the meat in the sandwich' or 'stuck in the middle' when conflicts between separated parents overflowed out of the child's home and into the early childhood setting. Many respondents wrote of the importance in such situations of maintaining boundaries and resisting being drawn into taking sides. The teacher who provided the following account was one of the 61% of respondents who reported that the Code of Ethics booklet was an important reference point in such situations. She noted that her training had "instilled" in her a regard for the Code of Ethics as a "tool to facilitate and manage sometimes difficult situations". She wrote about feeling:

> caught in the middle between conflicting parties over the custody of a child. Mother has emotional concerns; the father and the mother's parents' are all wanting the best for the child but [were] unable to reach agreement over these issues, including which party has the child, when and for how long.We remained impartial and as professional as possible, lending an ear to hear both sides' views without siding with either. We encouraged all parties to consider the best interests of the child (Education and care respondent).

In this situation, "not taking sides" meant that the teachers "lent an ear" to all the people involved so that the relationships with the home adults were not damaged, at the same time as the teachers advocated with them for "the best interest of the child". This balancing of relationships and consideration of the rights of all involved was characteristically present in teachers' responses in custody situations. The following example from a kindergarten respondent provides another illustration of this approach:

> Dad refused to give the child back after weekend access. He then brought the child to the kindergarten during the following week. It was a dilemma in terms of supporting the family in the most appropriate way. This involved carrying on as usual for the child. We referred to the Code of Ethics booklet [and] sought advice from the senior advisory teacher. We sought to act in the best interests of the child and not get involved in the custody battle (Kindergarten respondent).

For the teacher who reported this situation, referring to the Code of Ethics and seeking advice from a senior colleague provided guidance on how the competing demands of "support for the family" and acting "in the best interests of the child" could be handled. In a response to a question later in the survey, this teacher explained more fully the guidance she found in the Code when she referred directly to two values (value 13 and value 5) that she had found helpful. She wrote: "the

Code clearly states that teachers are an advocate for the child [value 13] and that they have a right to be emotionally safe [value 5]". With this guidance the teacher was able to untangle the normally straightforward professional obligation of "supporting the family" which was suddenly complicated by family adults who were at odds with each other.

Keeping relationships in balance, ensuring that children are able to maintain a relationship with both parents despite parental separations, and at the same time offering secure, stable experiences within the early childhood setting to support children during times of stress and change, were key goals that respondents aimed for in articulating the strategies they used in responding to difficult custody situations. One respondent wrote of "being very careful not to share information with either party that may have a detrimental effect on the child's relationship to mum and dad" (Education and care respondent, 1044) thus reflecting one of the Code's values that children are entitled to "have a relationship with both parents even when parents live apart, unless precluded by legal constraints" (value 15).

Example 2: Concerns about children's safety and well-being

Even more troubling for early childhood practitioners were situations that raised concerns about children's safety, health, and well-being. The following situation is typical of a number that were reported where it became clear to the teachers that children were in serious danger of abuse but where their attempts to follow procedures to protect the child did not lead to the desired result:

> We had a situation where 2 children were in a fostering situation that was not thought to be appropriate. There were 12 children in the foster care [home], one a known paedophile, and 24 hour supervision was required. The children would turn up [at the centre] inappropriately dressed, frightened of the foster father; the foster mother was never seen. Both the police and SES (Special Education Services) expressed their disapproval to CYFS (Child, Youth and Family Service) in writing and verbally, as did our centre. Nothing was acted upon by CYFS. The father had a criminal record etc. It was very frustrating especially when 2-and-a-half years later all the children were finally removed after an older girl notified authorities of sexual abuse. It was not made public and kept under wraps. [It was] very frustrating as we could have avoided the trauma to these children if we had been listened to. We went to our senior teacher, the police, wrote to CYFS etc. We kept fighting for the children's rights and giving them love and support as appropriate. (Home-based respondent)

In the example above, the inaction of CYFS (the government agency whose role it is to intervene in the lives of children and young persons when safety is an issue) rendered the carefully-taken actions of the early childhood practitioners ineffective. In New Zealand, teachers are not legally obliged to report concerns over child abuse though interagency protocols clearly make such reporting a professional ethical obligation. Thus, the teachers' decision to contact CYFS would have been seen as a major one flowing from a professional ethical obligation, rather than a legal responsibility. In this context, the inaction of CYFS is seriously troubling for people who are in a position of care over children. In the following example, CYFS was again cited as responsible for jeopardising a child's well-being through a breach of confidentiality after similarly carefully-thought through action by the early childhood team. A Playcentre[10] respondent wrote:

> [We had observed] severe neglect of a child over several months; we had big ethical discussions of [possible] ways forward. Unfortunately once our team decided on a course of action, the child was removed from the centre and help couldn't be given because CYFS broke confidentiality in telling the parent where the issue came from, whereas the centre was keen to provide a caring environment. Contact with CYFS was carried out after much debate; [there was] a consultation focused on child well-being and outcomes for child. Unfortunately the breach in confidentiality did not result in improvement (Playcentre respondent).

In commenting on the extent to which the Code had been useful in dealing with this situation, the respondent described how her playcentre team had worked with the Code "in a team situation to analyse all views and possible outcomes. [We] did not expect [the] child to be removed. The Code helped people understand all the ramifications and ensured all agreed on a course of action". This same respondent also wrote that "using the code of ethics supports my practice and decision making in dilemma situations. Also, it helps me look at situations from a variety of points of view, along with possible consequences".

In the next example, the duty of care can be seen to weigh heavily on the early childhood practitioners who attempted to provide care and support in a situation that was troubling, not only because of the clear distress experienced by the child and mother, but also because of the possible impact on other centre families of observing the extra attention and care that the teachers were giving to the family:

> The child ... comes daily in a very dirty state: clearly un-bathed and wearing the same clothes for several days. Mum is 17 years old and is clearly struggling. Dad is abusive and a restraining order is in place. Our dilemma was how much 'extra" assistance we were able to offer without upsetting other centre families. The centre bathed and fed the child each evening, and each morning we changed his clothes and washed and dried them. Child was fed breakfast each day (Education and care respondent).

Undeniably, the practitioners who provided these examples were guided in their actions by considerations of 'doing the right thing', both in terms of procedures as well as in terms of what children had a right to. At the same time, we interpret the respondents also being motivated by their duty of care and a desire to act in the best interest of all involved. In most of these cases, explicit reference to the Code of Ethics was clearly helpful in discerning what 'the right thing' was.

Example 3: Parental concerns about the impact of special needs children in centres – whose rights to meet first?

Another area of early childhood practice cited by respondents as causing difficult situations related to parental anxieties about their children "missing out" or being put at risk from behaviours exhibited by children with special needs. One Playcentre respondent commented that, in raising their concerns, parents often made demands on the early childhood team that brought to the fore "a dilemma between the rights of the child [special needs or otherwise] to participate in the programme and the need to ensure physical and emotional safety for the other children" (Playcentre respondent, 1504). This comment, which draws on two values listed in the Code of Ethics (value 2: the right of children to participate in all curricular experiences; and value 5: the right of children to be emotionally, psychologically and physically safe), illustrates yet again the guidance provided by the Code to early childhood practitioners. In the words of this respondent, referring to the Code helped the team by "reminding us about all children having rights".

Other respondents likewise reported dealing with parental concerns over other children's behaviours by reminding them that all children have a right to participate in early childhood education. One respondent, who noted the value of the Code of Ethics especially "in staff meetings ... in the decisions over children and parents/whanau", wrote:

> We have a special needs child with behavioural problems. Parents watch, listen and talk amongst themselves. They have concerns about the colourful language [of the special needs child] and his interactions with their children. [We] find it can be difficult as to whose needs need to be met first. [To resolve this] a teacher's aide has been employed for the three days he attends. [We've been] trying to explain to parents that the special needs child has rights too; they are now seeing an improvement in his behaviour and show more understanding (Kindergarten respondent).

This short account does not make explicit the full extent, and complexity, of the actions that the teachers in this kindergarten would have needed to put in place to transform the parental unrest into an eventual understanding of the special needs child. Such work is intense relationship work where rights and obligations have to be balanced with sensitivity to people's views, and even fears, and interactions have to be handled with care and respect.

Care and respect did not exclude firm action. A teacher in another kindergarten who wrote about the importance of showing respect to parents, also wrote about the need for firmness and direct speaking, and for basing action on "the child as the main consideration" (Kindergarten respondent, 1314). This teacher noted that in her kindergarten the Code was referred to "if staff are unsure of the ethics involved". She described one situation in which a number of parents put pressure on the kindergarten about the behaviour of a special needs child and threatened to withdraw their own children:

Other parents were discussing the behaviour of a violent rude child at kindergarten behind the back of the child's parents and teachers. Then they told the teacher they might withdraw their children if the situation continued. We informed the parents [that] the child has special needs and told them the matter was being dealt with by Group Special Education and that the child has a right to attend. Maybe (the kindergarten will) have teacher aide hours extended. I show[ed] the complaint procedure outline on display (Kindergarten respondent).

Such forthrightness takes courage and can be risky in complex situations that are troubling for all participants. Tempered with care and respect, forthrightness and courage emerged nonetheless as essential qualities among the full range of skills that early childhood practitioners used in their professional practice.

Example 4: Mismatch between policies and the needs of families

A final set of illustrations of the complex and competing demands of early childhood practice is drawn from situations that reveal the mismatch that can occur between the intentions of government policies and their impact on families. In these cases, early childhood practitioners bear the brunt of the mismatch and find themselves having to choose between acting in support of the "letter of the law" as prescribed in policy, or following a course of action that attends more specifically to the human context of the policy. To do the latter often means forfeiting the policy 'reward'.

A clear example of such competing demands arose from the ongoing focus in New Zealand early childhood policy on promoting increased participation in quality early childhood education services. The policy makes particular mention of Māori and Pasifika children whose rates of participation in early childhood services are lower than for other ethnic groups (Ministry of Education, 2002; Ministry of Education, 2007). In a separate policy, under funding rules, early childhood centres are required to apply strict criteria around monitoring attendance in order to claim funding for children. Teachers in different kindergartens reported their difficulty with this latter policy, particularly for families from the backgrounds where the Ministry is trying to raise participation rates. One kindergarten teacher wrote about the difficulty of:

The Ministry of Education rules about absences and 9+12 rule[11] etc. In a multi-cultural setting it is extremely hard. On one hand the Government is trying to get as many Pacific Island and Māori children into centres. Then they make all these stupid attendance rules and these specific children and families are the ones missing out: They have to be removed from (the attendance) list. This is a major concern (Kindergarten respondent).

The 'frequent absence' funding rule was also problematic for Playcentres with under-2 ½ year old children attending the sessions. One Playcentre respondent wrote:

[We have] parents with babies not arriving on time and/or leaving early because the baby cannot cope with a two-and-half-hour session. Therefore the centre cannot claim funding for them. [But] if they stay, everyone becomes upset! So, we support the parent and child by telling them to go home - we see the child's needs for sleep as paramount to everyone's sanity. We tell them to keep coming and gradually, as the child grows, the centre will be able to claim funding for them, when they can cope with the two–and–a-half-hour session (Playcentre respondent).

The respondents in both the above examples chose to respond to the human relational context of the policy rather than forcing the human context to fit into the policy, and thus forfeited the higher funding that enforcing attendance on the families would have rendered. Faced with the competing pulls of a legal requirement and the caring thing to do within their specific contexts, for each respondent it was their relationships, their detailed knowledge of the context, and care for the people involved in the context that won out. This was expressed very powerfully by the same Playcentre respondent later in the survey when, after commenting (as did the kindergarten teacher previously quoted) that the Code of Ethics could be used to "stimulate thinking regarding a particular issue and help clarify the best solution to the problem". This Playcentre respondent added:

But frankly, common sense prevails and you use your gut feeling or instinct. I have worked for 25 years and have been in the centre where I work now for 8 years. I believe I know my families and if you have a good relationship with the families, you don't need a book to tell you what to do.

This is an interesting comment, not the least because it is an elaboration of a statement about the usefulness of the Code as a guiding document. It suggests that while the Code was undeniably perceived as a useful and helpful tool of practice by this respondent (and others), this respondent was clear that choices about the best thing to do cannot ignore the lived experience of the relationships within which early childhood practice unfolds. The importance of understanding local context when making difficult professional decisions has a close parallel in the need for professional learning to be understood as a highly contextualised activity (see also Georgeson, this volume).

EARLY CHILDHOOD WORK AS INEVITABLY ETHICAL: NEW WAYS OF THINKING ABOUT PROFESSIONAL PRACTICE AND LEARNING

The examples discussed in the preceding section were intended to illustrate the complexity of early childhood practice, the fundamental link between professional learning and local practice, and the troubling nature of some of the difficulties that early childhood professionals encounter, an argument mounted also by Feeney and Freeman (1999) in North America, and Newman (1998) and Woodrow (2002), among others, in Australia.

At the time of developing the New Zealand Early Childhood Code of Ethics, we envisaged that practitioners would seek guidance from the Code to help them untangle the complexities and thus use the Code as a tool of learning and practice. In the supporting booklet for the Early Childhood Code of Ethics for Aotearoa/New Zealand (Early Childhood Code of Ethics National Working Group, 2001), we explained this vision:

> The existence of the code of ethics makes a public statement about our professional status, and demonstrates our determination to uphold the highest standards of ethical responsibility and conduct. The code of ethics is a statement of standards of ethical practice that the profession aspires to and abides by – a statement all early childhood educators agree on. When a problem or dilemma arises, the code can be referred to for guidance – but it cannot supply answers or solutions. There are no answers that apply across the board and no easy solutions. The code is a compass, not a map: it points out the direction but we have to choose our own path (p. 9).

This statement can be interpreted to suggest that the Code of Ethics project in New Zealand can be theoretically linked to more than one tradition of ethical scholarship. For instance, there is a direct link with the traditional view that Codes of Ethics are statements of rules and principles (Harris, 1994; Kultgen, 1988), which establish "norms against which to judge what is right or wrong, good or bad, normal and not normal" (Dahlberg & Moss, 2005, p. 68). Dahlberg and Moss and others (e.g. Harris, 1994) have argued that, viewed in this way, codes are consistent with a universalistic ethical approach associated with the German philosopher Immanuel Kant. In this approach, the focus is on formulating higher order principles or criteria that can form the basis of a contractual model of functioning within society (May, 1988) because "obligations and rights are closely connected, two sides of the same coin" (Dahlberg & Moss, 2005, p. 67). Translated to the context of early childhood work, this would mean that, from a Kantian perspective, having a code of ethics based on principles and standards of practice would be expected to create a contractual relationship between society and early childhood practitioners. In this contract, early childhood practitioners would be obliged to use the Code and uphold its ethical principles while society would be obliged to trust and respect them as individuals guided by standards of practice that confer on them professional status. As we noted earlier, such a 'contractual' outcome was one of the explicit aims of the Code of Ethics project; it set out to claim the ground of professional status for the early childhood sector in relation to New Zealand society.

In another link to Kantian traditions the difficult situations we have cited in this chapter suggest that the New Zealand Code of Ethics is indeed being used for guidance and as a tool of practice. In particular, the discussion of the practitioners' responses to the difficult situations reveals that the respondents' processing of the situations was in tune with the discourse of rights that is used in the New Zealand Code of Ethics. For example, some rights-based values utilised by the respondents were:

– the right of children to participate in all curriculum experiences (value 2);
– the right of children to "have their individual needs met" (value 3);

- the right of children to "be emotionally, psychologically and physically safe" (value 5);
- the right of children to "have adults advocate on their behalf" (value 13);
- the right of children to "have a relationship with both parents even when parents live apart unless precluded by legal constraints" (value 15);
- the right of parents to "support in their parenting/caregiving role" (value 22);
- parents' right to "equitable treatment unless precluded by legal considerations (eg: custody arrangements)"(value 26), and,
- parents' right to "have their personal circumstances respected" (value 28).

Thus, it is reasonable to claim that in using the Code of Ethics as a tool of practice, early childhood practitioners in New Zealand have adopted a rights-based discourse that could locate them within the philosophical camp of universalistic ethics associated with Kant.

But to link the practitioners' responses only to a Kantian tradition would be an incomplete analysis of what practitioners' accounts of their responses to difficult situations reveal about the nature of current early childhood professional practice in New Zealand. Furthermore, it would also overlook the statements in the extract from the Code of Ethics booklet quoted at the start of this section. For, in calling the Code 'a compass, not a map' and asserting that 'there are no answers that apply across the board and no easy solutions', the door is opened to another, newer tradition of ethical scholarship that is less about prescriptive rules and much more about negotiated solutions in specific contexts. Woodrow (2002) has called this a "situated ethics" approach and describes it as "involving the negotiation of relationships in particular sites and contexts" (p. 68). Woodrow highlights the indebtedness of this newer tradition to feminist ethics (e.g., Noddings, 1984; Tronto, 1999) and to new directions in applied ethics (e.g., Winkler & Coombs, 1993; DeMarco & Fox, 1986). Dahlberg and Moss (2005) have recently further linked this tradition to "postmodern ethics" (Bauman, 1993), in which the turn away from universalistic views of right and wrong has given way to a focus on themes such as "responsibility, relationships, situatedness, and otherness" (Dahlberg & Moss, 2005, p. 69). Noting the influence of Lithuanian philosopher Emanuel Levinas (1906 – 1995) and Polish social theorist, Zygmut Bauman (p. 1925) within postmodern views of ethics, Dahlberg and Moss include among its characteristics the tendency to:

> ...foreground wisdom, which involves an active practice to decide what is the best in a concrete situation. They engage with particularities and emotions rather than seeking the dispassionate application of general and abstract principles. They recognise the uncertainty, messiness and provisionality of decision making. Implicit in this turn to active ethical practice is trust in the ethical capacities of individuals, their ability to make judgements rather than simply apply rules (2005, p. 69).

In discussing practitioners' responses in the previous section of this chapter, we argued that, at the same time as being guided by considerations of 'doing the right thing', practitioners were also motivated by their duty of care, their concern for relationships, and by considerations of what would be in the best interest of all involved. Clearly, this ethics is not simply an ethics of rights and obligations, but rather an ethics that reflects the relationship-rich context of early childhood work. One of us (Cherrington, 2000) has already argued that the data from the 1994 survey revealed that an ethic of care (e.g., Noddings, 1984; Tronto, 1994, 1999) was at work in the way that early childhood teachers responded to difficult situations even at a time when the Code of Ethics was not yet in existence. In our view, the data from the 1994 survey makes clear that early childhood work is essentially relational work, a point cogently argued by Woodrow (2002) in her study of how ethical issues encountered in daily work were discussed and treated by a group of early childhood leaders. Woodrow concluded that her study provided "insights into the centrality of human relationships in early childhood work and how questions of ethics are fundamentally related to the interpretation and negotiations of these relationships" (p. 257). Our analysis of the data from the 2004 survey, ten years after the introduction of the New Zealand Code of Ethics, leads us to a similar conclusion. In the practitioners' attentiveness to relationships it is clear that, at the level of lived experience, professional early childhood practice is about maintaining intact a complex web of relationships in which, in the words of Dahlberg and Moss (2005), "ethical dilemmas arise not from conflicts of rights but from conflicts of responsibilities" (p. 76).

By arriving at this conclusion, our findings lead us to a view of early childhood ethical practice that is not simply, or primarily, about the balancing of rights in an attempt to achieve desired outcomes. Instead, we propose that our findings about the complex relational work inherent in early childhood practice suggest that, at a time of heightened interest in what it means to be professional in early childhood education (e.g., Adams, 2005; Dalli, 2006a; Karila, 2005; Urban, 2005) it is timely to foreground this complexity and re-vision professional practice as a new form of ethical practice. In this newly-visioned view of professional practice, the ethics that apply are not simply those enshrined in a Code of Ethics. Rather, the ethics of early childhood professional practice are rooted also in the ethics of care, concern for relationships, and wise regard for what would work best in a specific context (Winkler & Coombs, 1993; Woodrow, 2002).

In turn, this leads us to propose that this view of ethical professional practice calls for a new kind of professional learning: one that positions care, relationships, and wisdom as central to professional practice.

RE-VISIONING PROFESSIONAL LEARNING AS ETHICAL ACTIVITY IN A TIME OF CHANGE: WHAT COULD IT MEAN?

In an article on learning to develop as early childhood professionals, Australian early childhood scholar Jillian Rodd (1997), noted New Zealander Anne Meade's (1995) injunction that teachers need to be warm demanders of learning and competence when working with young children. Rodd also argued that the notion be applied to the learning of teachers themselves, urging early childhood practitioners to move beyond good practice to quality practice by becoming active in their own learning, so that they might influence change for the better. Rodd was arguing for a transformational agenda for the early childhood sector that would make early childhood teachers agents of change rather than passive recipients of it.

In similar vein, another Australian, Glenda MacNaughton (2005), has argued for transformation in asking her readers to imagine the types of change that could be possible when early childhood practitioners become part of "critically knowing early childhood communities" (pp. 188–213) (see also Blaise, this volume). MacNaughton explained "critical" by citing Foucault's rhetorical questions about the nature of philosophical activity:

> What is philosophy today – philosophical activity, I mean – if it is not the critical work that thought brings to bear on itself? In what does it consist, if not in the endeavour to know how and to what extent it might be possible to think differently, instead of legitimating what is already known? (Foucault, 1985, p. 9, cited in MacNaughton, 2005, p. 188)

Writing from a European perspective, Mathias Urban (2007, 2008) has recently proposed the concept of "a critical ecology of the profession" (see also Dalli, 2007). Noting the changing and uncertain context of the early childhood field, as practice and as a sociological phenomenon, Urban draws on the ideas of Donald Schön to argue that practitioners make sense of uncertain situations through "reflective conversations" with the situations; through these conversations, the situations are re-framed, understood and changed. Urban argues that a new paradigm of early childhood professionalism is needed in which professionalism is seen as an activity of creating understandings and co-constructing knowledge through interactions in complex socio-ecologic contexts (see also Edwards, this volume). Included in this paradigm is the notion of professionalism, and professional learning, as a relational concept. Building on this argument, Urban (2008) urges the promotion of a critical ecology that is "informed by the political and social realities that produce knowledges and practices, 'together with the use of this knowledge to strategically transform education in socially progressive directions' (MacNaughton, 2003, p. 3)" (cited in Urban, 2008, p. 146: italics in text).

In this chapter we too have had a transformative agenda: We have sought to bring thought to bear on itself and to explore how it might be possible to think differently about professional learning. We have done this by reflecting on what early childhood practitioners have said about how they have dealt with difficult situations in their local professional context and asked ourselves what this could mean for the type of professional learning that is needed in a time of change.

We have concluded, as others have argued (Feeney & Freeman, 1999; Newman & Polnitz, 2002; Woodrow, 2002), that early childhood professional practice is troubling, complex, and embedded in relationships. There is no reason to suppose that learning about professional practice should not be the same. By looking closely at the ways that practitioners have used the New Zealand Code of Ethics in dealing with troubling situations, we have argued that it is necessary to expand our understanding of the ethics involved in early childhood professional practice. In this expanded understanding, the ethics involved are derived from the everyday realities of early childhood work and speak not only of rights and competing values but incorporate notions of care, relationships and wise practice. We see this argument as a transformative one for professional learning and practice because, conceptually, it moves early childhood ethics away from universalistic models of ethical thinking and towards postmodern views that take account of the complexities of modern times, times marked by uncertainties and change (Bauman, 1993; Lyotard, 1984; Urban, 2008).

Politically too, this argument is potentially transformative: This is because by making it possible to see ethics as not only guided by principled statements of rights but as also related to notions of care, relationships and wise practice, it is possible to engage in creating a new discourse of professionalism, one that is more responsive to the lived realities of early childhood practice (see also Dalli, 2006a; Urban, 2008). Inevitably this raises questions about the validity of ethical codes over time; about the applicability of codes across diverse contexts within a given professional system; and about whether ethical codes should be revised to ensure currency and to reflect new realities and new professional discourses. Likewise, there are questions to explore about the connection between our proposed notions of care, relationships, and wise practice as elements of ethical practice and professional learning, and arguments about professional virtues and self-regulation by a profession (May, 1988). Although it is not the purpose of this chapter to engage with these questions, we wish to at least provoke them, since we see them as flowing naturally from our argument and trust that they will be addressed elsewhere.

From the perspective of the task of this book we suggest that, in the attempt to conceptualise professional learning in relation to the changing world of early childhood, we must position care, relationships, and wisdom as central elements in professional learning aimed at promoting ethical professional practice. Forms of professional learning that take account of the new ethics of professional practice are, for us, the new frontier of professional learning.

NOTES

[1] The NZ curriculum document Te Whāriki was released in draft form in 1993 and finalized in 1996.
[2] In September 2002, the Ministry of Education launched Pathways to the Future: Ngā Huarahi Arataki, a 10-year strategic plan for early childhood. The document describes early childhood education as the "cornerstone of our education system" which benefits "our social, educational and economic health" (Ministry of Education, 2002, p. 1).
[3] Parts of this story appear also in Dalli, C. (2003a). Early childhood policy in New Zealand: stories of sector collaborative action in the 1990s. Education International Working Papers no 10.
[4] This has since been re-named Early Education Federation.
[5] IGC grant V212/451/RGNT/594/602 awarded through Victoria University of Wellington.
[6] The Early Childhood Development Unit (ECDU) was a government agency set up in the late 1980s as the operational support and professional development arm of Government for the early childhood sector. It was re-named Early Childhood Development in 1998. In 2003 it was disestablished as an independent unit and incorporated within the Ministry of Education.
[7] Whānau is a Māori word equivalent to family/extended family.

[8] Tangata whenua translates from Māori as 'people of the land' or the indigenous people of a country.

[9] In 1994, the Combined Early Childhood Union of Aotearoa (CECUA) merged with the New Zealand Educational Institute (NZEI), the primary teacher's industrial union, to become NZEI Te Riu Roa, a joint union that covers early childhood and primary school teachers.

[10] Playcentres are licensed and funded early childhood services operated by a national network of parent co-operatives.

[11] The "9+12 rule" is one of a set of regulations designed to ensure that places for individual children are not funded for more than the legal entitlement when children attend more than one service, or when children experience frequent absences, or there are changes in enrolment.

REFERENCES

Adams, K. (2005, September). *Whàt's in a name?* Paper presented at the European Early Childhood Education Research Association conference, Dublin, Ireland.

Bauman, Z. (1993). *Postmodern ethics.* Oxford: Blackwell Publishers.

Bourdieu, P., & Passeron, J.-C. (1977). *Reproduction in education, society and culture* (R. Nice, Trans.). Beverly Hills, CA: Sage.

Cherrington, S. (2000). *Beyond the physical: An ethic of care in early childhood.* Unpublished MEd thesis, Victoria University of Wellington.

Cunningham, J. (1993). *Habitus and misrecognition.* Ontario Institute for Studies in Education. Retrieved January 4, 2005, from http://www.ed.uiuc.edu/EPS/PES-yearbook/93_docs/CUNNINGH.HTM

Dahlberg, G., & Moss, P. (2005). *Ethics and politics in early childhood education.* London: RoutledgeFalmer.

Dalli, C. (1993). Is Cinderella back in the cinders? A review of early childhood education in the early 1990s. In *New Zealand annual review of education* (Vol. 3). Wellington: Victoria University of Wellington.

Dalli, C. (2003a, September). Early childhood policy in New Zealand: Stories of sector collaborative action in the 1990s. *Education International Working Papers* No. 10.

Dalli, C. (2003b, September). *Professionalism in early childhood practice: Thinking through the debates.* Paper presented at the 13th European Early Childhood Education Research Association annual conference, University of Strathclyde, Glasgow.

Dalli, C. (2006a). Re-defining professionalism in early childhood practice: A ground-up approach. Views from teachers in care and education settings. *Early Childhood Folio, 10,* 6–11.

Dalli, C. (2006b). Re-visioning love and care in early childhood: Constructing the future of our profession. *The First Years: Nga tau tuatahi, 8*(1), 5–11.

Dalli, C. (2007, September). *Towards a critical ecology of the profession.* Symposium paper presented at the 17th European Early Childhood Education Research Association annual conference, Prague, Czech Republic.

Dalli, C., & Cherrington, S. (1994, December). *Survey of ethical concerns faced by early childhood educators in Aotearoa/New Zealand: Preliminary results.* Paper presented at the New Zealand Association for Research in Education conference, Christchurch.

Dalli, C., & Mitchell, L. (1995, September). The early childhood code of ethics or How you can prise yourself from between a rock and a hard place. Keynote address. *The Proceedings of the 6th Early Childhood Convention, 1,* 63–76.

Dalli, C., & Te One, S. (2004). Early childhood education in 2002: Pathways to the future. In I. Livingston (Ed.), *New Zealand annual review of education* (Vol. 12, pp. 177–202). Wellington: Victoria University of Wellington.

DeMarco, J. P., & Fox, R. M. (1986). *New directions in ethics. The challenge of applied ethics.* New York: Routledge and Keegan Paul.

Duncan, J. (1998). *I spy: Sexual abuse prevention policies. Protection or harm? A kindergarten case study*. Presentation for the Institute for Early Childhood Studies (IECS). Wellington: Institute for Early Childhood Studies.

Early Childhood Code of Ethics National Working Group. (2001). *Early childhood code of ethics for Aotearoa/New Zealand*. Wellington: NZEI Te Riu Roa. ISBN 0908579-45-4

Feeney, S., & Freeman, N. (1999). *Ethics and the early childhood educator. Using the NAEYC Code*. Washington, DC: National Association for the Education of Young Children.

Harris, N. (1994). Professional codes and Kantian duties. In R. F. Chadwick (Ed.), *Ethics and the professions* (pp. 104–115). Aldershot, England: Ashgate Publishing.

Karila, K. (2005, September). *A Finnish viewpoint on professionalism in early childhood education*. Paper presented at the European Early Childhood Education Research Association conference, Dublin.

Kipnis, K. (1987, May). How to discuss professional ethics. *Young Children*, 26–30.

Kultgen, J. (1988). The ideological use of professional codes. In J. C. Callaghan (Ed.), *Ethical issues in professional life* (pp. 411–421). Oxford: Oxford University Press.

Lange, D. (1988). *Before five: Early childhood care and education in New Zealand*. Wellington: Department of Education.

Lyotard, J.-F. (1984). *The postmodern condition: A report on knowledge* (G. Bennington & B. Massumi, Trans.). Manchester: Manchester University Press.

MacNaughton, G. (2005). *Doing Foucault in early childhood studies. Applying poststructural ideas*. New York: Routledge.

May, H. (2001). *Politics in the playground. The world of early childhood in postwar New Zealand*. Wellington: Bridget Williams Books/NZCER.

May, H. (2007). 'Minding', 'working', 'teaching': Childcare in Aotearoa/New Zealand, 1940s–2000s. *Contemporary Issues in Early Childhood*, 8(2), 133–143.

May, W. F. (1988). Professional virtue and self-regulation. In J. C. Callaghan (Ed.), *Ethical issues in professional life* (pp. 408–411). Oxford: Oxford University Press.

Meade, A. (1988). *Education to be more: Report of the early childhood care and education working group*. Wellington: Government Print.

Meade, A. (1990, November). Women and young children gain a foot in the door. *Women's Studies Journal*, 97–110.

Meade, A. (1995). *Good practice to best practice*. Keynote address at the Start Right '95 conference, Royal Society for the encouragement of the Arts, Commerce and Manufacture, London.

Meade, A., & Dalli, C. (1991). Review of the early childhood sector. *New Zealand Annual Review of Education*, 1, 113–132. Wellington: Victoria University of Wellington.

Ministry of Education. (2002). *Pathways to the future: Ngā huarahi arataki*. Wellington: Learning Media.

Ministry of Education. (2007). *Ka Hikitia – Managing for success: The draft Māori education strategy 2008–2012*. Wellington: Ministry of Education.

Mitchell, L. (1995). Crossroads – Early childhood education in the mid-1990s. In *New Zealand annual review of education* (Vol. 5, pp. 75–92). Wellington: Victoria University of Wellington.

Newman, L. (1998, September). *Taught or caught? Ethics for professional practice in early childhood teacher education courses*. Paper presented at the eighth annual conference of the European Early Childhood Education Research Association. Santiago di Compostela, Spain.

Newman, L., & Pollnitz, L. (2002). *Ethics in action. Introducing the ethical response cycle*. Canberra: Australian Early Childhood Association.

Noddings, N. (1984). *Caring: A feminine approach to ethics and moral education*. Berkeley, CA: University of California Press.

Robinson, A., & Stark, D. (2002). *Advocates in action*. Washington, DC: NAEYC.

Rodd, J. (1997). Learning to develop as early childhood professionals. *Australian Journal of Early Childhood*, 22(1), 1–5.

Smith, L. (1993). Government's role in early childhood. Speech notes of the Minister of Education. In *What is Government's role in early childhood education? Proceedings of the NZCER seminar.* Wellington: NZCER.

Tronto, J. (1994). *Moral boundaries. A political argument for an ethic of care.* New York, London: Routledge.

Tronto, J. (1999). Caring: gender-sensitive ethics. *Hypatia, 14*(1), 112–120.

Urban, M. (2005, September). *Dealing with uncertainty: Approaching the dilemma of an autonomous early years' profession.* Paper presented at the European Early Childhood Education Research Association conference, Dublin, Ireland.

Urban, M. (2007, September). *Towards a critical ecology of the profession.* Symposium paper presented at the 17th European Early Childhood Education Research Association annual conference, Prague, Czech Republic.

Urban, M. (2008). Dealing with uncertainty: Challenges and possibilities for the early childhood profession. *European Early Childhood Education Research Journal, 16*(2), 135–152.

Wells, C. (1999). Future directions: Shaping early childhood education policy for the 21st century – A personal perspective. In *New Zealand annual review of education* (Vol. 8, pp. 45–60). Wellington: Victoria University of Wellington, School of Education.

Winkler, R., & Coombs, J. (Eds.). (1993). *Applied ethics: A reader.* Oxford: Blackwell.

Woodrow, C. (2002). *Living ethics in early childhood context: A critical study.* Unpublished PhD thesis, Central Queensland University.

Associate Professor Carmen Dalli
Director, Institute for Early Childhood Studies
Victoria University of Wellington
Sue Cherrington
Institute for Early Childhood Studies
Faculty of Education
Victoria University of Wellington

SUSAN EDWARDS

6. BEYOND DEVELOPMENTALISM

Interfacing professional learning and teachers' conceptions
of sociocultural theory

INTRODUCTION

This chapter draws on research conducted by the author into teachers' uses and understandings of sociocultural theory as an alternative paradigm for conceptualising learning and development, to a cognitive-constructivist approach. Professional learning is examined in relation to research methodologies that draw on and respect teachers' existing professional knowledge as the starting point for learning and for the generation of conceptual change. A framework for understanding the transition points in teachers' thinking, regarding the differences between the developmental and sociocultural paradigms is outlined and used as basis for examining issues provoked by the increased use of a sociocultural perspective in early childhood education for both children and teachers.

THE POST-DEVELOPMENTAL NATURE OF CONTEMPORARY EARLY CHILDHOOD EDUCATION

Contemporary perspectives in early childhood education and care have tended to employ a post-developmental discourse in which assumptions about the normative and objective basis of developmentalism and its role in early education have been questioned. Work emanating from the reconceptualist movement throughout the latter part of the twentieth century brought together a conceptual framework for critiquing developmentalism. Drawing on feminist, critical, post-modernist, post-structural and multicultural perspectives, these critiques provided an avenue for constructing understandings about children, childhood, growth and development that moved beyond those presupposed by developmentalism (Ball & Pence, 2000; Soto & Swadener, 2002, p. 38), particularly as expressed in the theory-practice relationship articulated by the Developmentally Appropriate Practice Guidelines (Bredekamp & Copple, 1997). Two simultaneous movements were of importance, including the increased recognition in Western academia of the importance of Vygotsky's cultural-historical theory to interpretations of development (Daniels, 1994); and movement within the sociological literature towards the notion of 'new childhoods' (Prout, 2005). The intersections between the reconceptualist movement, cultural-historical theory and 'new childhoods' have contributed to the growth of a contemporary perspective for understanding childhood that challenges the presence of a universal description for development and focuses instead on

S. Edwards, J. Nuttall (eds.), Professional Learning in Early Childhood Settings, 81–95.

understanding and interpreting the contexts of childhood, development and learning.

Internationally, this view is increasingly evident in formalised curriculum documents, position statements, and research literature that draw on sociocultural theory, new conceptions of childhood and postmodernist ideals to describe child development as culturally determined and children's participation in their communities as a function of their human rights. This movement is evident in the Organisation for Economic Co-operation and Development (OECD) Starting Strong II report into early childhood education and care, where the social pedagogy tradition (including educational approaches from countries such as Sweden, Norway, Denmark, Italy and Germany) describes childhood in terms of rights and community participation:

> The child as a subject of rights: autonomy, well-being, the right to growth on the child's own premises. The child as agent of her/his own learning, a rich child with natural, learning and research strategies. The child as member of a caring community of peers and adults, in which the influence of the child is sought. An outdoors child of pleasure and freedom. A time for childhood that can never be repeated (OECD, 2006, p. 141).

Other documents likewise privilege post-foundational perspectives and describe new understandings of childhood and development as central to the work conducted in early education and care settings (for example New Zealand/Aotearoa's *Te Whariki*; Sweden's *Curriculum for the Pre-School*; and Scotland's *Curriculum Framework for Children 3 to 5*). Across Australasia, post-developmental perspectives have in part drawn on interpretations arising from sociohistorical theory, with a particular emphasis on the works of Vygotsky. Here, knowledge construction has been defined as inseparable from the social and cultural practices in which it is enacted and created (Vygotsky, 1929/1994). The extent to which the available Australasian curriculum documents adequately reference this perspective has been questioned (Nuttall & Edwards, 2007); however they nonetheless represent a shift from the previously dominant developmental discourse. For example:

> Social constructivist approaches to learning recognise the child as a co-constructor of meaning and knowledge. These approaches build on neo-Piagetian research and the work of Vygotsky, and recognise that the child's construction of meaning and understanding is mediated and modified by social interactions within their families, communities and environments (Department of Education, Training and Employment, 2001, p. 6).

> The adult's role is to actively encourage and support [children] on their voyage of possibility – adults who are open to their ideas, who listen and are willing to share the learning process with them. When both adults and children possess an optimistic outlook, together they can actively create opportunities and possibilities that might previously have been 'unexpected and unimagined' (Stonehouse, 2002: cited in Moore, 2006, p. 13).

According to Fleer (2003), the transition from developmentalism to sociocultural theory is one amongst many of the changes in perspective associated with post-developmentalism in early education. The significance this shift holds for how children's learning is perceived by teachers, and consequently how curricula are constructed, has been canvassed at a theoretical level (Anning, Cullen & Fleer, 2004; Edwards, 2003; Farquhar & Fleer 2007; Nuttall & Edwards, 2007; Walsh, 2005). However, research into teachers' uses of sociocultural theory over the traditionally valued developmental perspective suggests the need to further understand how existing theoretical ideas are utilised by teachers as reference points for interpreting newer theoretical perspectives (Fleer & Richardson, 2004; Fleer & Robbins, 2004).

UNDERSTANDING THE THEORY-PRACTICE RELATIONSHIP AND APPROACHES TO PROFESSIONAL LEARNING

Research regarding early childhood teachers' understandings about the relationship between theory and practice has moved beyond attempts to match teacher's professed theoretical beliefs to observable practices in the classroom. Rather, contemporary perspectives on the theory-practice relationship highlight the complexity of teachers' contextual experiences and the manner in which these experiences are utilised as a framework for interpreting theory in relation to practice (Nuttall & Edwards, 2004). Understanding the theory-practice relationship as contextually defined reduces the emphasis on the notion of the gap between theory and practice. This allows contextual issues to be seen as factors that influence both practice and the selection of theory that informs practice. This view reduces the need for professional learning aimed at eliminating the perceived gap between theory and practice. Korthagen (2001) argues that working from the gap perspective serves only to entrench a technical-rationalist interpretation of theory in which the teacher's role is to implement the theory as given, rather than mediating theory, practice and experience (see also, Kessels and Korthagen, 2001). Research conducted by the author (Edwards, 2004) into early childhood educators' perceptions of Developmentally Appropriate Practice (DAP) supports this view. In this study, teachers were asked to develop metaphors for their interpretations of DAP and its relationship to practice. The author suggested that teachers interpreted the theoretical content embedded in DAP in relation to practice, and that even a rejection of the theory represented an act of consideration that served to coalesce rather than separate theory and practice:

> The act of consideration functions as a bridge between the theory and practice, possibly suggesting that the 'gap' is closely related to the particular interpretation an individual educator places on *how* the theory relates to practice. Whether or not this theory is aligned with the nominated approach is irrelevant, since the very act of consideration has operated as bridge between the two in any instance. It is possible that previous descriptions of the gap

actually represent an assumption that the educator has managed to misalign her practice with the curriculum approach, rather than acknowledging that she has possibly shaped her practice in considered opposition to the approach's described theoretical imperatives (Edwards, 2004, p. 95, italics in original).

Rejection of the 'gap' as a concept for explaining the relationship between theory and practice opens up significant opportunities to redefine and reconsider what professional learning is from a philosophical perspective. In other words, seeing theory and practice as contextually defined means professional learning begins with the understandings teachers hold about children's learning, rather than the belief that teacher development is best served by one-day workshops where "in-servicing represents an action done to teachers, rather than something spring[ing] naturally from their own views of personal development" (Campbell, 2003, p. 375). The literature associated with early childhood teacher professional learning thus focuses on a particular interpretation of the teacher-as-practitioner-as-learner (otherwise known as the teacher-researcher) and approaches to learning that draw on a range of methodological perspectives including, action research (Carr, May, Podmore, 2002; Kemmis & McTaggert, 1988), developmental work research (Engestrom, 1999), reflective practice (Pring, 2000) and collaborative research (Fleet & Patterson, 2001a; Ronnerman, 2005). Broadly speaking, the focus is on understanding the teacher and his/her practice within his/her given context. This involves the application of new theoretical concepts to existing practice in order to discover new ways of understanding teaching and learning and therefore approaching practice. Typically, professional learning is conceived as most appropriate and effective in situations where teachers are encouraged to draw on their existing understandings of theory in the conceptualisation of new material:

> Research needs to become embedded in the practical-knowledge of the community of practitioners and inform practitioners' ways of seeing and being as they work with clients. At the same time, it needs to be sensitive to the existing values and expertise, that is, cultural capital, that practitioners already bring to bear on their professional decision making (A. Edwards, 2000, pp. 16–17).

These approaches value the situated nature of teacher knowledge and use them as a basis for engaging in professional learning that generates conceptual change. This argument suggests such change is more likely to influence pedagogical decision making than a focus on change at the procedural level alone:

> There is now an extensive stock of empirical data which attests to the effectiveness of achieving meaningful change by addressing teachers' existing knowledge, beliefs and practice. This process has been conceptualised as self-sustaining generative change which does not involve acquiring a set of procedures for uncritical implementation, but entails teachers making changes in their basic epistemological perspectives, their knowledge of what it means

to learn, as well as their conceptions of classroom practice. (Wood & Bennett, 2000, p. 636)

These approaches to professional learning begin with teacher knowledge and seek to develop new knowledge in a way that displaces not only the notion of the gap, but also the very pedagogical practices that might be derived from its existence (for example, top-down, theory-driven professional development). Rather, experiential knowledge is positioned in relation to theoretical knowledge, which in turn enables the theoretical to operate as a means of understanding, interpreting and critiquing practice (Moss, 2005). The teacher actively researches his/her own conceptualisation of the teaching and learning process within her educational context, and in doing so, is positioned more strongly as an expert engaged in professional learning than a 'student' attending professional development.

CONTEMPORARY APPROACHES TO PROFESSIONAL LEARNING AND THE APPROPRIATION OF SOCIOCULTURAL THEORY BY EARLY CHILDHOOD EDUCATORS

Contemporary approaches to professional learning, such as teacher-research, developmental work research and collaborative research have been important in investigations aimed at understanding how early childhood educators use sociocultural theory in practice (see for example Edwards, 2007b; Fleet & Patterson, 2001a). The historical position held by developmentalism across Australia (despite the production of socioculturally based curriculum documents), has resulted in the situation whereby many practitioners still draw on a developmental discourse to inform their understandings of children's development and learning (Fleer & Robbins, 2004, p. 47). The implementation of professional learning experiences aimed at challenging teacher's existing conceptions of development in relation to the ideas emerging from sociocultural theory have therefore necessitated respect for existing knowledge. In doing so, these studies have drawn on a range of professional learning methodologies to support teachers interested in making the transition from developmentalism to sociocultural theory (see for example, Fleet & Patterson, 2001b). Although in its infancy in the Australasian context, research surrounding the developmental-to-sociocultural transition suggests that sociocultural theory is met with initial resistance by pre-service and practicing teachers as an informant to their practice (Fleer & Richardson, 2004; Fleer & Robbins, 2004). These findings suggest that the modernist perspective defines development so strongly that opportunities for the developmental process to be considered in any other terms are limited (Burman, 1994; Edwards, 2005; Fleer, 2003). Time to absorb new ideas and opportunities to explore sociocultural theory in practice have been considered central to teachers' appropriation of an alternative theoretical perspective and conceptions of development (Edwards, 2006a). Whilst these findings are consistent with the arguments associated with contemporary approaches to professional learning, more knowledge is needed to understand *how* the transition is processed according to the central tenets held by both developmentalism and sociocultural theory. In other words, how do teachers move from a developmental to sociocultural perspective in terms of understanding the theoretical imperatives of each theory in relation to the professional learning experience itself?

Research conducted by the author (Edwards, 2006b, 2007a & 2007b) addresses this question and shows how teachers' initial resistance to sociocultural theory can be understood as part of the process of moving from a developmental-to-sociocultural perspective. The professional learning experience has been shown to be crucial to this process and suggests that resistance may be viewed as a commitment to developmentalism that characterize a teacher's interpretation regarding particular 'truths' about development (Edwards, 2007b). Examination of an alternative paradigm (such as sociocultural theory) allows the 'truth' expressed by developmentalism to be challenged and enables teachers to think in new ways about development; reducing their initial resistance to the ideas embedded within an alternative theoretical framework. This in turn provides an avenue for teachers to think about learning and development in new ways and opens opportunity for culture to be seen as the origins of, rather than influence on, development.

A FRAMEWORK FOR UNDERSTANDING TEACHER THINKING

Two separate studies conducted over a 12-month period (Edwards, 2006b; 2007a & 2007b) have attempted to contribute to understandings regarding how teachers engage with sociocultural theory. This research has led to the development of a framework for understanding the transition points in teacher thinking when teachers engage with sociocultural theory as an alternative paradigm for understanding development. Both projects involved early childhood educators working in a collaborative research relationship with the author to examine their existing conceptions of developmentalism in relation to their understandings of curriculum. During each of these projects, sociocultural theory was presented as an alternative theoretical framework to developmentalism, and used as a means of problematising developmental theory (A. Edwards, 2001; S. Edwards, 2003; Fleer, 2003; Robbins, 2005). Project one primarily employed a collaborative research methodology (Edwards, 2006b), whereas project two employed a developmental work research approach (Engestrom, 1987) and engaged teachers in the direct application of sociocultural theory to practice (Edwards, 2007a & 2007b). Common findings from the projects suggest commonalities in the transition from developmentalism-to-sociocultural theory, in which teachers are seen to move through four phases of thinking, each characterised by a particular aspect of the professional learning process. These phases are identified in the framework for understanding teacher thinking presented in Table 1 and discussed in detail with reference to research data cited in Edwards (2006a, 2007a and 2007b) in the following sections of this chapter.

Table 1. Framework for understanding teacher thinking: key phases involved in the developmental-to-sociocultural transition in relation to the professional learning process

Phase	Developmental-to-sociocultural transition point	Associated professional learning aspect
1.	Existing beliefs about learning and development expressed in predominately developmental and constructivist terms	Begins with a focus on existing beliefs, views, theories and philosophies. What are these? Why are they held? Why do they matter?
2.	Initial familiarisation with sociocultural theory sees teachers defining 'culture' as a function of difference between cultural communities due to a customary commitment to developmentalism	Sociocultural theory introduced into a professional and pedagogical context which positions developmentalism as a customary way of viewing development and learning
3.	Continued investigation of sociocultural theory shifts the focus from one of cultural difference to one where culture is seen as a context for learning and development	Examination of an alternative theoretical perspective highlights the notion that developmentalism does not represent a truth about development and that development can be culturally rather than normatively defined.
4.	Understanding culture as a context for learning disables the status quo associated with developmental norms and enables new interpretations of learning to be articulated that focus on interactions in learning and peer-to-peer engagements. These interpretations provide a basis for moving beyond respect for cultural difference to understanding the role of culture in children's learning, and therefore children's ability to access the curriculum provided by teachers.	Focuses on opportunities to discuss the implications of the new theory, test the theory in practice, gather data related to the testing and share data and findings. Involves reflection, critique, reading, research and questioning of practice and the relationship between the sociocultural perspective and teaching practice

UNDERSTANDING THE DEVELOPMENTAL-TO-SOCIOCULTURAL TRANSITION

Phase one of the developmental-to-sociocultural transition is strongly related to teachers' existing beliefs, views and values regarding early education and development. Both projects regarding teachers' interpretations of sociocultural theory commenced with an examination of their existing views and values in a manner consistent with those articulated by the contemporary professional learning literature (Edwards, 2000; Wood & Bennett, 2000). In these sessions, teachers were asked to explain their philosophical positions on early education, to write these in reflective journals and consider how they viewed children's development and learning. Invariably, these descriptions were developmental in orientation, drawing on the notion of developmental norms, Piagetian-informed approaches to learning and the need to plan for individual children. For example:

> My philosophy is that all children have individual needs and develop at different stages. This means the curriculum comes from the children. Their interests/needs/wants are met by planning play-based experiences (Teacher two).

> The program is play-based and based on the observed needs, interests and developmental progress of the children (Teacher four).

> The curriculum is child-centred, initiated, directed and adult supported. It considers all developmental areas – social, emotional, cognitive and physical. It should be flexible (Teacher seven).

In such cases, participating teachers had been presented with developmentalism in their initial teacher education as the main theoretical perspective for interpreting development and learning. Consequently, developmentalism tended to be viewed as the norm for informing practice and, in the manner identified by Burman (1994), represented a common sense truth about childhood, more so than it did a particular perspective on development as a human phenomenon. For example:

> Piaget was the theory that I remember most from university and I believe that the ages and stages gave me the basis of where a child should be when I needed guidance and ideas as a beginning teacher. Even though children are very different and move through the stages at different rates it was comforting to be familiar with these stages (Teacher three).

During the professional learning episodes teachers' existing beliefs and values were used as the starting point for professional learning. This meant that developmentalism was represented as the customary vehicle for thinking about the nature of childhood, development and learning. The introduction of sociocultural theory into this context results in the second identified phase in the developmental-to-sociocultural transition, whereby culture is perceived as a function of difference between communities. In this phase, teachers discuss sociocultural theory using developmentalism as their reference point for understanding the sociocultural argument. During this phase, developmentalism maintains its position as a 'truthful' theory for teachers, meaning that sociocultural theory is interpreted *in relation* to developmentalism, rather than as a theoretical explanation in its own right (Edwards, 2005). This means teachers understand the cultural aspect of sociocultural theory as referencing different cultures, rather than as an operant of developmental progress within a given cultural context (Rogoff, 2003). For the teachers, understanding sociocultural theory in this manner après to results in two particular responses, both of which derive from the original commitment to developmentalism. In the first response, teachers claim to be 'already doing sociocultural theory' by respecting differences amongst children and by 'looking at individuals and groups' (Edwards, 2007b, p. 7). This response builds largely on the teachers' existing conceptions of development and represents a 'confirmed' reaction to the introduction of sociocultural theory whether or not the reaction is sociocultural in its interpretation (Edwards, 2007b, p. 12). In the second response, teachers view sociocultural theory as a justification for cultural diversity rather than a theoretical perspective on development. Here, teachers use sociocultural theory to explain the complexities associated with working with multicultural communities. For example, one teacher outlined the issues associated with the arrival of a new child from Afghanistan:

> I've got a child at the kinder at the moment who is from Afghanistan and they speak Farsi and she doesn't speak any English at all. Understands some to a small degree. But the amount of assistance the other children provide to her is just amazing (Teacher four).

This interpretation is not inherently disrespectful, deliberately resisting of a new perspective, or even theoretically misguided. Rather, because it is made in relation to the developmental perspective held by teachers, it seeks to explain the alternative offered by sociocultural theory within an existing conceptual framework. Phase three of the developmental-to-sociocultural transition is crucial at this point and involves teachers understanding, via the continued examination of sociocultural theory as an alternative theoretical perspective, that development-alism does not necessarily represent a 'truth' about development (in fact anymore so than sociocultural theory). This process is difficult, and as teacher discussion shows, involves simultaneous attempts to release and maintain developmentalism as an explanatory mechanism for practice:

> Piaget's theory has been promoted all the way through University so questioning his concepts/relevance has been a little daunting. Piaget's theory still has some relevance in providing guidelines although we must take in account culture, today's society, families in particular, and environmental considerations (Teacher four).

> This session helped me to focus on the different cultures we work with – different values. How do we incorporate these differing values into our programs? We value children's independence and ability to do things themselves – compared to Sri Lankan children who are still dependent on their parents, e.g. preschool children still spoon-fed – this is how parents show their love and caring, our way would appear uncaring. It we dismiss Piaget altogether what is left? (Teacher eleven)

As teachers come to understand that developmentalism may not explain the developmental experiences of all children and that sociocultural theory positions cultural participation as a defining construct in development they begin to view sociocultural theory as alternative theoretical perspective in its own right. An insightful reflection by one teacher regarding her work with Somalian children highlights the nature of the third phase:

In some cultures there are things that children have just never experienced in any way, shape or form. They might be really interested when they first see it but they have no knowledge to bring to that table. The Somalian communities I worked with, these children had never seen scissors or toys. They actually climbed the walls and tables because they had never been in that [preschool] environment. I tried doing things [to support the children] but even that was from a white perspective, like I put out little black dolls and they would have played with a stick for hours. So they come to a traditional western kindergarten which is foreign in its expectations of how you play – you know, do you play with a stick or do you play with a computer? So what are you doing to those children? Does Piaget's theory actually work for those children? (Teacher eight)

From this point forward, teacher thinking tends to centre on understanding *culture as the context* for learning and development representing the fourth phase in the developmental-to-sociocultural transition. In this phase, the status quo assumed by developmental norms is challenged by the understanding that developmentalism does not necessarily represent a truth about children's growth and learning. Rather, the realisation that learning can be conceptualised in means other than developmental allows new interpretations of learning to be articulated which focus on the role of interactions between children and adults in learning. Once this transition point is reached, teachers tend to discuss learning as culturally constructed and socially mediated. References to individual development were used to explain the difference between the developmental and sociocultural perspectives, rather than as a starting point for understanding sociocultural theory itself. For example:

My philosophy now is focusing more on the quality of interactions between children and adults. I believe now in looking and observing children in groups rather than focusing on the individual. Looking at prior notes, I didn't really take into account how important and vital the interactions with their peers are. I still strongly value positive and rich learning environments but the project has also made me think and reflect on my practices interacting with children. Like what questions to ask? Where do ideas come from? And the importance of scaffolding between adult-to-child and peer-to-peer (Teacher five).

My philosophy now would include acknowledgement of the child's cultural values and beliefs and how important peers and interactions are in the learning process of children; scaffolding, collaboration and interactions. I have a deeper understanding of what culture actually means. We all have our own culture. I never thought this way before (Teacher nine).

Central to this fourth phase is the finely tuned distinction between valuing culture and social interactions as the means for learning, compared to respecting them as adjuncts to a developmentally-based approach to learning. Teachers operating in the fourth phase view learning as socially and culturally constructed in a manner which enables them to reflect on how their programming and planning decisions impact on children's capacities to access the intended learning associated with their curriculum. Teachers report thinking more critically about children's socially and culturally mediated forms of learning and how these are enabled or silenced in their classroom according to their previously held beliefs about normal development and normal ways of learning in early childhood education:

> Really stopping and thinking when you are interacting and making decisions or making assumptions or whatever, 'how much of this is my value, my thinking, my understanding and how much is real or true to that child? Like, how much is my value as opposed to what be might be the values of that child, that family or whatever? (Teacher fourteen)

> I think [the project] has deepened my understanding in different ways of different places. For example, the depth of the cultural impact on children's learning. I knew it was important, but it sort of deepened my understanding and broadened it in different areas. Like I sort of did agree that it was important to recognise and look at different cultures and treat them with respect but it has broadened my understanding of why it is so important. It is about the listening, like before it was OK for children, but now it is more OK. I thought that it was better for children to participate and that was the desired outcome for them – to join in and participate. But really a lot of the learning I have realised comes to them just by looking and watching and seeing the interaction and listening. So I respect it more (Teacher five).

These realisations involve teachers thinking about what they are offering young children and why. Working from a sociocultural perspective contrasts the developmental orientation in which children were previously described by teachers has 'having individual needs and developing at different stages'; and curriculum positioned as 'play-based and based on the observed needs, interests and developmental progress of the children' (Teachers two and four). Children's social and cultural experiences are seen as mediators of the developmental process, and teachers become more alert to the culturally valued forms of learning children bring to their classrooms. In doing so, teachers reflect more carefully on the implications of the nature of cultural development and understand that sociocultural practice is not so much about respecting cultural difference as it is about understanding the reciprocity between children's social and cultural experiences and the pedagogical worlds within their classroom walls.

CONCLUDING COMMENTS: FUTURE ISSUES IN SOCIOCULTURALLY
INFORMED EARLY CHILDHOOD EDUCATION AND PROFESSIONAL LEARNING

Movement beyond technical-rationalist understandings of the relationship between theory and practice have emphasised the need for early childhood professional learning to begin with the knowledge, values and experiences teachers hold as a means of generating meaningful change to their practice. The research examined in this chapter was based on this premise, and involved teachers in an initial consideration of their current knowledge and values with respect to early education. This aspect of professional learning has been shown to contribute to teachers' willingness to engage in the conceptual development associated with the developmental-to-sociocultural transition. In other words, beginning with teacher beliefs provides space for developmentalism to be examined as the core belief system, and enables sociocultural theory to be introduced as an alternative theoretical perspective. Had existing beliefs been ignored and sociocultural theory introduced as an alternative perspective, the likelihood is that the central tenets of sociocultural theory would simply be assimilated to the existing developmental framework. This would have reduced the opportunity for practice to be orientated towards understanding how social and cultural participation shapes children's experiences of the early childhood program. To be effective, professional learning aimed at supporting teachers in their use of sociocultural theory has to begin with their existing theoretical and practical understandings of the teaching and learning process. In doing, professional learning can work to challenge the concepts associated with developmentalism in a manner that moves beyond valuing culture in a multicultural sense to seeing cultural participation as the crucible for learning and development.

Two potential issues require consideration regarding the application of sociocultural theory as (one of many available) post-developmental perspectives associated with teacher learning in early childhood education. Firstly, as the groundswell of reading, research and opinion grows around the suitability of sociocultural theory as an informant to early education, care will need to be taken to ensure that professional learning experiences are appropriately informed by opportunities for existing beliefs around development to be examined. Failure to do so runs the risk of sociocultural theory being assimilated to developmentalism within the early childhood profession. Should this happen, the potential for the theory to operate as a system for generating reflexively informed (rather than technical-rationalist based) practice will be reduced. This will be evidenced in publications and descriptions of practice that claim learning is 'socially and culturally situated' in much the same way developmental-constructivism is now represented by the catch-cry 'children learn through play.' Sophisticated understandings of sociocultural theory will be necessary to avoid this outcome and to promote the possibilities associated with this theoretical perspective for informing practice.

Second, if development and learning are characterised across the profession as culturally determined, how this concept will be interpreted and related to practice requires consideration. This issue centres on which cultural practices will come to be most valued in early childhood education; those of the learners themselves, or those traditionally forming the foundations of curriculum? If those of the learner are privileged the potential exists for sociocultural theory to transform early childhood education so that children's social and cultural experiences form the basis of curriculum decision making. Conversely, if value continues to be placed on the existing cultural practices (as drawn from the developmental-constructivist paradigm), sociocultural arguments may well be appropriated as a means of explaining current pedagogical practices. Here sociocultural theory may be justified to help children adjust to the existing pedagogical climate, rather than actually transforming pedagogy in relation to an alternative perspective on the nature of learning and development. Whether or not sociocultural theory will be utilised to transform early education, or whether early education will transform sociocultural theory remains to be seen. How this question will be answered depends on how early childhood professional learning is to be developed, funded and implemented during the next ten to twenty years. Whatever the answer, the situation will necessarily lead to the need for new research and understandings regarding how teachers work with, and understand, post-developmental perspectives such as sociocultural theory in relation to their practice.

REFERENCES

Anning, A., Cullen, J., & Fleer, M. (2004). Research contexts across cultures. In A. Anning, J. Cullen, & M. Fleer (Eds.), *Early childhood education. Society and Culture* (pp. 1–19). London: Sage Publications.

Ball, J., & Pence, A. (2000). A postmodernist approach to culturally grounded training in early childhood care and development. *Australian Journal of Early Childhood, 25*(1), 21–25.

Bredekamp, S., & Copple, C. (1997). *Developmentally appropriate practice in early childhood programs* (Rev. ed.). Washington, DC: National Association for the Education of Young Children.

Burman, E. (1994). *Deconstructing developmental psychology*. London: Routledge.

Campbell, A. (2003). Teachers' research and professional development in England: Some questions, issues and concerns. *Journal of In-service Education, 29*(3), 375–388.

Carr, M., May, H., & Podmore, V. (2002). Learning and teaching stories. Action research on evaluation in early childhood in Aotearoa-New Zealand. *European Early Childhood Education Research Journal, 10*(2), 115–125.

Daniels, H. (1994). The individual and the organisation. In H. Daniels (Ed.), *Charting the agenda. Educational activity after Vygotksy* (pp. 46–106). London: Routledge.

Department of Education, Training and Employment. (2001). *South Australian curriculum standards and accountability framework*. Carlton South, Victoria: Curriculum Corporation.

Edwards, A. (2000). Research and practice: Is there a dialogue? In H. Penn (Ed.), *Early childhood services. Theory, policy and practice* (pp. 184–199). Buckingham: Open University Press.

Edwards, A. (2001). Researching pedagogy: A sociocultural agenda. *Pedagogy, Culture and Society, 9*(2), 161–186.

Edwards, S. (2003). New directions: Charting the paths for the role of sociocultural theory in early childhood education and curriculum. *Contemporary Issues in Early Childhood, 4*(3), 251–266.

Edwards, S. (2004). Teacher perceptions of curriculum: Metaphoric descriptions of DAP. *Australian Research in Early Childhood Education, 11*(2), 88–98.

Edwards, S. (2005). Talking about a revolution: Paradigmatic change in early childhood education. From developmental to sociocultural theory and beyond. *Melbourne Studies in Education, 46*(1), 1–12.

Edwards, S. (2006a). *Interfacing action research and professional development: Exploring the learning opportunities afforded to practitioners via a Preschool Philosophy Document*. Paper presented at the 10th annual New Zealand Research in Early Childhood Education conference and symposia, 4th–5th December, Porirua City, New Zealand.

Edwards, S. (2006b). 'Stop talking about culture as geography.' Early childhood teachers' conceptions of sociocultural theory as an informant to curriculum. *Contemporary Issues in Early Childhood, 7*(3), 23–252.

Edwards, S. (2007a). From developmental-constructivism to sociocultural theory and practice: An expansive analysis of teachers' professional learning and development in early childhood education. *Journal of Early Childhood Research, 5*(1), 89–112.

Edwards, S. (2007b). Theoretical transitions and professional learning: How do early childhood teachers understand sociocultural theory? *New Zealand Journal of Early Childhood Education, 10*, 131–144.

Engestrom, Y. (1987). *Learning by expanding: An activity-theoretical approach to developmental research.* Helsinki: Orineta-Konsultit.

Engestrom, Y. (1999). Activity theory and individual social transformation. In Y. Engestrom, R. Miettinen, & R. Punamaki (Eds.), *Perspectives on activity theory* (pp. 19–39). Cambridge: Cambridge University Press.

Farquhar, S., & Fleer, M. (2007). Developmental colonisation of early childhood education in Aotearoa/New Zealand and Australia. In L. Keesing-Styles & H. Hedges (Eds.), *Theorising early childhood practice: Emerging dialogues* (pp. 27–51). Baulkham Hills, NSW: Pademelon Press.

Fleer, M. (2003). Early childhood education as an evolving community of practice or as lived social reproduction: Researching the taken-for-granted. *Contemporary Issues in Early Childhood, 4*(1), 64–79.

Fleer, M., & Richardson, C. (2004). *Observing and planning in early childhood settings: Using a sociocultural approach.* Canberra: Early Childhood Australia.

Fleer, M., & Robbins, J. (2004) 'Yeah that's what they teach you at Uni, it's just rubbish': The participatory appropriation of new cultural tools as early childhood student teachers move from a developmental to a sociocultural framework for observing and planning. *Journal of Australian Research in Early Childhood Education, 11*(1), 47–62.

Fleet, A., & Patterson, C. (2001a). Professional growth reconceptualised: Early childhood staff searching for meaning. *Early Childhood Research and Practice, 3*(2), 1–13.

Fleet, A., & Patterson, C. (2001b). Professional development: Perceptions of relevance. *Journal of Australian Research in Early Childhood Education, 8*(1), 61–70.

Kemmis, S., & MacTaggart, R. (1988). *The action research planner* (3rd ed.). Geelong: Deakin University.

Kessels, J., & Korthagen, F. (2001). The relation between theory and practice: Back to the classics. In F. Korthagen (Ed.), *Linking practice and theory. The pedagogy of realistic teacher education* (pp. 20–32). Mahwah, NJ: Lawerance Erlbaum.

Korthagen, F. (2001). Teacher education: A problematic enterprise. In F. Korthagen (Ed.), *Linking practice and theory. The pedagogy of realistic teacher education* (pp. 1–20). Mahwah, NJ: Lawerance Erlbaum.

Moore, L. (2006). *Building waterfalls. A living and learning curriculum framework for adults and children (birth to school age).* New Market, Queensland: Crèche and Kindergarten Association.

Moss, P. (2005). Structures, understandings and discourses: Possibilities for re-envisioning the early childhood worker. *Contemporary Issues in Early Childhood, 7*(1), 30–41.

Nuttall, J., & Edwards, S. (2004). Theory, context and practice. Exploring the curriculum decision-making of early childhood teachers. *Early Childhood Folio. A Collection of Recent Research, 8*, 14–18.

Nuttall, J., & Edwards, S. (2007). Theory, policy, and practice: Three contexts for the development of Australasia's early childhood curriculum documents. In L. Keesing-Styles & H. Hedges (Eds.), *Theorising early childhood practice: Emerging dialogues* (pp. 3–25). Baulkham Hills, NSW: Pademelon Press.

Organisation for Co-operation and Economic Development. (2006). *Starting strong II. Early childhood education and care.* France: OECD Publishing.

Pring, R. (2000). *Philosophy of educational research.* London: Continuum.

Prout, A. (2005). *The future of childhood.* London: Routledge Farmer.

Robbins, J. (2005). Brown paper packages? A sociocultural perspective on young children's ideas in science. *Research in Science Education, 35*, 151–172.

Rogoff, B. (2003). *The cultural nature of human development.* Oxford: Oxford University Press.

Ronnerman, K. (2005). Participant knowledge and the meeting of practitioners and researchers. *Pedagogy, Culture and Society, 13*(3), 291–312.

Soto, L., & Swadener, B. (2002). Toward liberatory early childhood theory, research and praxis: Decolonising a field. *Contemporary Issues in Early Childhood, 3*(1), 38–66.

Vygotsky, L. (1929/1994). The problem of the cultural development of the child. In R. Van Der Veer & J. Valsiner (Eds.), *The Vygotsky reader*. Oxford: Blackwell.

Walsh, D. (2005). Developmental theory and early childhood education: Necessary but not sufficient. In N. Yelland (Ed.), *Critical issues in early childhood education* (pp. 40–49). Berkinshire: Open University Press.

Wood, E., & Bennett, N. (2000). Changing theories, changing practice: Exploring early childhood teachers' professional learning. *Teaching and Teacher Education, 16*(5), 635–647.

ACKNOWLEDGEMENT

The author wishes to thank the project participants for their contributions to each of the projects represented in this chapter. Receipt of project funding from the City of Casey (2005 – 2006), and from a Monash University through a Staff Research Project Grant (2004) is also acknowledged.

Susan Edwards
Centre for Childhood Studies
Monash University

JOCE NUTTALL, LISA COXON AND SARAH READ

7. STRUCTURE, AGENCY, AND ARTEFACTS: MEDIATING PROFESSIONAL LEARNING IN EARLY CHILDHOOD EDUCATION

A Case Study of Two Preschool Teachers in Victoria, Australia

INTRODUCTION

In this chapter, we describe a recent small-scale professional learning project, based on collaboration between the three authors, in Melbourne, Victoria, Australia. The project took the form of regular professional learning 'conversations' and occasional workshops, with the broad aim of examining the relationship between sociocultural theory (Rogoff, 1998, 2003) and professional practice in Victorian preschools (kindergartens). Teachers' appropriation of sociocultural principles is not, however, the focus of this chapter. Instead, we discuss the unexpected insights we gained from these conversations into why professional learning in ECE is inevitably a complex and highly context-specific activity. In particular, the project highlighted the dynamic relationship between structure and agency in professional learning, and the mediating role of professional ideas and artefacts, designed in specific workplace settings, upon such learning. We develop this argument by first considering the relationship between teachers' learning dispositions and teacher agency, then by introducing the concept of structural quality (specifically, staff:child ratios) into the agency/disposition relationship. Finally, we drawn on Engeström's (1987) formulation of cultural-historical activity theory to argue that, by capturing some of the tensions and contradictions that inevitably arise between structure and agency in work settings, teachers can sometimes develop new and meaningful forms of professional practice in spite of everyday limitations.

BACKGROUND TO THE STUDY

The origins of the project

In the early 2000s, the final-year professional placement (practicum) unit in the early childhood degrees offered at Monash University, Melbourne, began to emphasise the utility of sociocultural theory (Rogoff, 1998, 2003) in constructing curriculum and pedagogy in early childhood settings. This initiative met with varying degrees of success in the early stages, with many of the preschool teachers supervising student placements being reluctant to engage with new theoretical perspectives (Fleer & Robbins, 2004).

S. Edwards, J. Nuttall (eds.), Professional Learning in Early Childhood Settings, 97–113.

Some teachers, however, were excited by the university's attempts to move beyond Developmentally Appropriate Practice (Bredekamp & Copple, 1997), which had been the dominant source of ideas about ECE programs in Victoria for many years (Edwards, 2003). These teachers wanted to know more but the university did not have the resources to offer widespread professional development about sociocultural theory.

Two teachers (and co-authors of this chapter) were particularly determined to learn more about socioculturally-influenced curriculum. So, in early 2005, the two teachers – Lisa Coxon and Sarah Read – began a two-year collaboration with Dr Joce Nuttall of Monash University, framed by an expectation of mutual benefit: Lisa and Sarah would receive regular, free, one-on-one professional development sessions; in exchange, they would allow their meetings with Joce to be taped and transcribed for research purposes.

The focus for the professional learning was determined entirely by the participating teachers. Although Lisa and Sarah began with a broad interest in the application of sociocultural theory, individual sessions quickly became focused on context-specific, needs-based issues, which Joce helped the teachers explore from a sociocultural perspective. The research investigation parallelling the professional development sessions was to be a fine-grained analysis of how preschool teachers appropriate new theoretical perspectives, the cognitive and behavioural shifts prompted by the meetings, and the factors that supported and/or hindered professional learning in preschools.

The research context

Preschools in Victoria, Australia, cater mainly for four-year-old children in the year prior to formal schooling. Most preschools are community-operated and sessional, with children attending two or three half-day sessions per week. Sarah teaches in exactly this type of preschool, a community-based kindergarten, in a middle-class suburb in south-east Melbourne. The preschool is operated by an active and hardworking parent committee, and Sarah has taught at the centre for several years. The preschool is completely stand-alone, with no oversight from a preschool association or local authority, other than being licensed by the state government. Two groups of four-year-old children attend the preschool, each group for three sessions per week, and there are 26 children in each group. A three-year-old group also attends the centre for one half-day each week but is not taught by Sarah, this timetable means Sarah has two half-days a week of non-child-contact time. Sarah is the sole-charge teacher, supported by one full-time assistant.

Lisa, by contrast, teaches in a small preschool in an, affluent suburb on the outskirts of Melbourne. Lisa's centre is attached to a private fee-paying school and she has close relationships with the campus Principal and other teachers, particularly in the Junior School. The same 19 children attend the centre from 9.00 am to 3.00 pm, four days a week. Lisa has two assistants, both qualified early childhood educators, and the children at the centre are also taught for a few hours per week by specialist teachers from the main school, in subjects such as music. At the time the project began, Lisa was also teaching a three-year-olds group on Fridays but, by the end of 2006, this group had been assigned to another teacher.

The research and development process

At the outset, Joce arranged to meet regularly (roughly once every two months) and individually with Lisa and Sarah. Although these meetings were framed as 'interviews', they were designed to be far more mutually beneficial than a traditional research interview. Each meeting began in the same way, with a 'catch up' about the goals set at the end of the last meeting and identification of how Lisa or Sarah wanted to benefit from this next session. Following Denzin's (2001) advice, that the best qualitative research interview is in the nature of a conversation, these regular meetings were largely conversational and perhaps best described as 'co-constructions'. In exploring issues around theory and practice, it was notable that each participant was assisting the other to construct *different* bodies of knowledge, drawing on complementary bodies of expertise: during the meetings, Lisa and Sarah were alert to their developing understanding of sociocultural theory, and discussed with Joce how they might explore it in their centres; Joce, by contrast, listened closely for accounts of shifts in Lisa and Sarah's thinking and practice, and also noted methodological or other issues for further investigation.

Although the project was designed as parallel case studies of two teachers, Lisa and Sarah's curiosity about each others' participation meant these conversations were soon supplemented by three-way meetings. By meeting together, Sarah and Lisa were able to identify topics of mutual interest (e.g. how best to report assessment information to parents). Where they felt they needed a less free-flowing approach to new ideas, Joce would run a workshop-style presentation for the two teachers, held on the University campus, in addition to the individual meetings. Using this simple design, the project proceeded for two years, until late 2006.

It would be a misnomer to describe this collaborative research and development process as a 'program', since this implies some kind of pre-determined content or outcome. Instead, Joce arrived each time at Lisa or Sarah's preschool without prior warning of the issues the teachers might be grappling with or the direction they wanted their learning to take. Joce sometimes supplied follow-up readings or other material for the teachers, and Lisa and Sarah also corresponded occasionally by email. After each meeting, the audio record was transcribed and returned to Lisa or Sarah, respectively, for their amendment or further comments. These transcripts were then open coded, with particular attention to key topics, evidence of shifts in the language being used by any of the three participants, accounts of tensions or difficulties in practice, and accounts of changes in thinking or in day-to-day practice. Lisa and Sarah have subsequently co-authored all publications from the project.

At one level, the project appears to be a form of 'mentoring'. However, traditional constructions of mentoring imply an imbalance between the expertise and insight of the mentor and mentee. Instead, Sarah, Lisa, and Joce brought their own particular expertise and interests to the project and the conversations were explicitly an exchange of ideas, rather than a transmission or supervision model. By making these agendas explicit from the start, the three research participants were able to explicitly claim *different* benefits from the project.

FINDINGS

This chapter discusses three themes identified during data analysis: the relationship between teachers' learning dispositions and teacher agency in professional learning; the ways cultural and historical structures afford or constrain teachers' learning in Victorian preschools; and the ways in which new professional ideas and artefacts can mediate the relationship between structure and agency to produce new forms of professional thinking and action.

Learning dispositions and teacher agency in professional learning

It was evident from the beginning of the project that Sarah and Lisa shared strong, positive, dispositions toward their own learning. This was reflected in their curiosity and persistence in expanding their knowledge of sociocultural theory, and was a theme of our early conversations. Mitchell and Cubey (op. cit) identified teachers' dispositions toward lifelong learning as an important factor in professional development outcomes. The present project attempted to dig deeper into the source of this orientation.

Learning dispositions are sometimes, incorrectly, conflated with attitudes or personality (Claxton, 1999), or with temperament or 'dispositions' in general, implying they are largely intrapersonal, and are developed and maintained by individuals. Instead, Carr and Claxton (2002) provide a socioculturally-oriented definition of dispositions as "... a tendency to edit, select, adapt and respond to the environment in a recurrent, characteristic kind of way" (2002, p. 13). Learning dispositions can be explicitly taught and are socially constructed, as an excerpt from the first meeting with Lisa suggests:

Joce ... Okay, ... are you able to think back to why you decided you wanted to be a teacher?

Lisa I don't know that it was ever actually a conscious decision. It was just always going to be. It was just always going to be young children and it was always going to be pre-school. I was always surrounded by young children. And they were always drawn to me.

Joce You know I am exactly the same. I couldn't tell you. There was never a conscious decision to become a teacher.

Lisa   It was always…

Joce   Yeah.

Lisa   … just in me.

Joce   And I did things like Sunday school classes and baby sitting and it was just always kids around and it just seemed natural that I would be a teacher, but I mean if you asked me that question I couldn't tell you either.

Lisa   It wasn't a decision.

Joce   Yeah.

Lisa   It was just who I was.

Lisa's point that she "was just always going to be" could imply an essentialist view of choosing to teach. However, Lisa's account of how children were "always drawn" to her belies the fact that the persistence and creativity necessary to engage with young children are not innate but *learned* through social processes.

Sarah had also made a commitment to be a preschool teacher from a young age:

Sarah I always wanted to be a kinder teacher. My mum was an assistant at my kinder so she was there when I was in four year old kinder. And so I had a lot of time at kinder and the teacher was very old school and came down hard on everyone, and she wasn't someone that I could approach or anything like that, and I just wanted to be an approachable kinder teacher.

Joce   This is when you were a child you were thinking that?

Sarah Yep.

Joce   Yeah. Gosh.

Sarah So, ever since school everyone knew that I wanted to be a kinder teacher and, yeah, I didn't deviate from that at all.

Sarah's comment that she "didn't deviate" from her path to teaching, identified at the age of four, suggests she learned how maintain her determination to achieve her goals from an early age. The conversations related here between Joce and Sarah, and Joce and Lisa, provide examples of how all three of the authors persisted from childhood with their goal of teaching. Clark (1995) also argues that powerful constructs of what it means to be a 'good' teacher, including the attitudes to learning that go with it, are frequently learned by observing one's own teachers during childhood.

But such histories are not sufficient to guarantee that teachers will make a strong commitment to *their own* lifelong learning in their chosen profession. Analysis of conversations with Lisa and Sarah suggest that teachers with a strong orientation toward ongoing learning have incorporated this feature *into their archetype* of a good teacher:

Joce [When I first met you and Lisa], what came through with both of you is that real passion for wanting to learn more and apply it...

Sarah I think that's one of the aspects of being a good teacher though. Always wanting to improve yourself and to learn more because you are there to teach the kids and learn from the kids so you've got to be a good learner yourself.

Joce So, you think that's a characteristic of a good teacher that they're into continuous improvement?

Sarah Yeah. Definitely. You've always got to develop.

It is perhaps self-evident that positive learning dispositions are an advantage in professional learning, but for professional learning to be sustained, learning dispositions such as persistence, creativity, risk-taking, and experimentation are particularly important (Sadler, 2002).

It is important, however, to also attend to factors beyond teachers' learning dispositions. Otherwise, we run the risk that teachers' orientation toward their own learning will be viewed as an entirely individual responsibility, particularly in the types of sole-teacher settings in which Lisa and Sarah work. An individualistic focus on professional learning overlooks the important systemic and contextual factors that frame teachers' work. Lisa and Sarah were able to identify these structural factors, but even they tended to situate the limits to their professional practice within themselves. However, analysis of data generated in this project suggests that the learning of teachers, children, and families in Victorian preschools is framed by persistent structural limitations, and that teachers must be highly agentic in their approach to their own learning. In the first part of this chapter we have focused on teachers' learning dispositions because, as the project progressed, it became increasingly clear that successful professional learning partly depends on the way in which positive learning dispositions *enhance teacher agency*. This is a theme we return to later in this chapter, but first we provide an example of how structural factors can afford or constrain professional learning.

Structural factors in preschool teachers' professional learning

A simple example of structural constraints is that of staff:child ratios. Ratios of staff to children in early childhood settings are an established indicator of structural quality in early childhood settings (Smith, Grima, Gaffney, Powell, Masse, & Barnett, 2000). In this project, however, it became evident that staff:child ratios were also a key variable in affording or constraining *teachers'* learning. Some of the benefits of Lisa's situation, as Director of an early childhood centre attached to a large private school, arose during an early interview:

Joce   So the best part about working in this Centre?

Lisa Uninterrupted time with the children. A small group, one small group of children as opposed to having to get to know fifty children in a short space of time. I've got, you know, this year I've only got nineteen children.

Joce   Fantastic.

Lisa   And I've got four days a week uninterrupted time.

Joce   With that nineteen?

Lisa   Quality time with those children.

Joce   And a day is nine til three?

Lisa   Uh huh.

Joce   Four days a week?

Lisa   Yep.

Joce   Awesome

Lisa   It's just fantastic and I've got fantastic support staff. They are just exceptional and I've got two of them. (Laughs).

Joce   I was going to say, yeah, nineteen and three adults is...

Lisa   Sensational.

Joce   Wonderful.

Staff:child ratios in Lisa's centre provide Lisa with "uninterrupted time" and "quality time", during which she can focus closely on the children's learning and development, and on the effects of changes in her pedagogical strategies.

By contrast, Sarah sometimes found the demands of teaching 52 children across the week highly frustrating. The group size and staff:child ratio of Sarah's preschool was an enormous constraint in trying to implement one of Sarah's goals in the project: the maintenance of meaningful individual assessment records for all 52 children. Early in the project, Joce tried to convince Sarah that her struggle wasn't due to personal failings but to structural problems arising from the cultural and historical form of preschools in Victoria:

Sarah [I read the book you gave me then thought], 'Oh my God, I'm a hopeless teacher.' (Laughs)

Joce   Oh no, why did you think that?

Sarah There was a part in here talking about active and passive teacher.

Joce   Yeah.

Sarah Page twelve, and I thought I am so a passive teacher. (Laughs). I just, I guess, yeah....

Joce   How do you interpret that? Like, what do you think passive teacher means?

Sarah I don't feel that I am picking up on their interests and needs as much as I could be doing. I don't think I'm making enough links in what I'm observing. I think I've got the observation part okay....

Joce   Yeah.

Sarah ...but I think it's the analysis and then the follow through and because I plan fortnightly I'm not modifying my programs. But I guess that the stressful thing with that is finding the time and the energy to actually do that.

Joce   Yeah.

Sarah And that's what I'm finding hard.

Joce   Yeah. Okay.

Sarah So that's why I'm interpreting myself as being a passive teacher.

(Both laugh).

Sarah Yeah.

Joce   Can I just say a couple of things about that?

Sarah Yep.

Joce   When I talk about passive teaching, in a large part that's dictated by the nature of preschool programs, not by you and your teaching style.

Sarah Mmm hmm.

Joce   It's actually the structural nature of program, [which] means that it's very difficult for you not to be a passive teacher, or to not, be as active as you would like. Because ... there's one of you and there's 26 children and this afternoon there's going to be a different 26.

Sarah Mmm.

Joce   So I think you need to cut yourself some slack at this point. That this is the way preschools are set up in Victoria, stop me if I've mentioned this before, [but] it's a historical artefact.

Sarah had internalised the idea that, because she was unable to keep up-to-date with her assessment records, that she was a "hopeless" teacher. Sarah gave several examples across her interviews of individual children needing her undivided attention for long periods during centre sessions. These, and other demands, reduced her time for working on areas where she wanted to develop, such as recording assessments and reflecting back to the children aspects of their learning. This meant that Sarah did not make the progress with her learning goals that she had hoped for, but she often blamed herself for not having achieved the tasks she set for herself, rather than viewing this as a logical consequence of the cultural and historical form of Victorian preschools.

The model of sessional preschools, with sole-charge teachers and high ratios of children to staff, is the dominant model in Victoria. Like many other places where the kindergarten movement began with the charitable activities of middle-class women in the 19th century, the structure of Victoria's preschools still assumes that there are large numbers of single women and mothers in the community with free time to devote to voluntary activities in the preschool, allowing the teacher to concentrate on curriculum and pedagogy. This historical form has proved remarkably persistent, and one reason for this may be that teachers who find the ratios and group size challenging conveniently construct themselves as 'hopeless', rather than questioning the historical and cultural structures they have to negotiate.

Negotiating the dynamic relationship between structure and agency

The relationship between structure (such as group size and ratio) and agency (including teachers' individual and collective curiosity and persistence) is not a simple dichotomy. Rather, structure and agency exist in dynamic tension. Teachers internalise the structural features of the preschool at the same time as they exert agency over them. In the remainder of this chapter, we explore how teachers can capitalise strategically upon the contradictions inherent in the structure-agency relationship, to learn new forms of practice.

One such strategy, identified during the project, arose in early 2007 when Sarah attended a one-day in-service course about portfolio-style assessment in early childhood settings. Sarah noted how a structural feature of Victorian preschools – the regulatory power of the Department of Human Services (now the Department of Education and Early Childhood Development) – appeared to limit teachers' learning. Until very recently, the Department of Human Services (DHS) administered the licensing regulations for early childhood services in Victoria. These regulations are somewhat vague with respect to planning, assessment, and reporting expectations but many teachers have internalised the idea that the DHS imposes rigid rules about curriculum planning and assessment (i.e. that reporting can only be individual and based on developmental norms) and that teachers who deviate from this prescription will be officially reprimanded. Sarah reported that, at the in-service course:

Sarah There was the same reaction yesterday [at the in-service course].

Joce Yeah?

Sarah Because they were hearing that stuff [about portfolio assessment] for the first time and they were saying, 'What about Human Services?

Joce [Sighs] Yeah, as they do.

Sarah And it was good of [the course facilitator] to say, "Yeah, well Human Services is fine. These are the Regs; you're still meeting the Regs."

Whilst the licensing regulations are a key structural feature of Victorian preschools, the limits on acceptable forms of assessment are not imposed by the

DHS but by teachers themselves, in the form of a 'rule' that has gained widespread cultural acceptance.

In his expansion of Vygotsky's claims about the role of cultural tools and artefacts in mediating the relationship between subject and object, Engestrom (1987) has argued that rules are an integral part of all activity systems (such as preschool provision), and that they serve to mediate the relationship between the subject (individual teachers) and the community (the early childhood field).

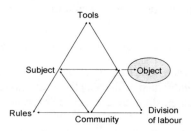

Figure 1. Engestrom's (1987) representation of the mediating role of tools, rules, and division of labour in relationships between subject, object, and community

Rules have enormous discursive power, since adoption or rejection of particular rules is a key part of how teachers express their subjectivities. In this case, by uncritically adopting the (cultural) rule that only certain forms of assessment practice are acceptable in Victorian preschools because of structural constraints (the regulatory power of the DHS), the teachers were also adopting limits to their risk-taking and, consequently, their professional learning. By contrast, Sarah had rejected this rule and was already engaging with new ideas about assessment. The threat of regulatory surveillance and punishment had lost its power to limit Sarah's experimentation. By identifying and working with the contradiction between her desire for more holistic assessment and the discursive rules about 'approved' approaches imposed by the DHS, Sarah was exerting her agency as a professional and repositioning herself amongst her colleagues.

An important shift for Sarah during the project had been to come to terms with structural aspects of the preschool that she could not change, and adapting her pedagogical tools accordingly. Around the time of the in-service course, Sarah said 'goodbye' to making detailed individual observations of children to reproduce in their individual portfolios (which she called 'Learning Journals'). Instead, Sarah used the (abstract) tools of sociocultural theory to design a (concrete) observation tool that would allow her to focus more on children's activities in groups, whilst still deriving individual information for the portfolios:

Sarah So, okay, that's it for the Learning Journal. No more Learning Journal. I'm going to do similar to what [I saw another teacher] doing. So, if there are groups that are doing, like, we've had a group that's been loving fairies a few weeks ago...

Joce Mmm.

Sarah ... I could have followed that along and extended that a lot. Well I, we, did extend it but [I could have] really documented it a lot more thoroughly in their conversations and include that in their portfolios instead. And then just have the observations that I was doing in the Learning Journal but doing it more on the computer, and it will look nicer, because that's been one of my concerns. And it will be a lot better I think.

Joce I sense a breakthrough here! (Laughs).

Sarah (Laughs). I think you wanted me to do that at the start, didn't you?

Joce (Laughs). No, not necessarily.

Sarah (Laughs). I had to get there myself.

Whilst some structural features of kindergartens are beyond teachers' immediate control, there are many ways in which teachers can take advantage of the multiple contradictions between structure and agency to devise new forms of practice. Critical reflection on seemingly rigid rules about knowing and doing are just one example.

The power of pedagogical tools in mediating professional learning

Another strategy, exemplified by Sarah's decision to redesign her observations, is the development of new pedagogical tools to mediate the relationship between subject (the teacher) and object (the learning and development of the children). During the project, the development of new pedagogical tools was an explicit focus for both Lisa and Sarah. Initially, these tools were mainly abstract, in the form of concepts drawn from sociocultural theory but, as the project progressed, Sarah and Lisa sought to concretise these ideas in the form of professional artefacts such as planning templates and assessment formats.

An early step for Sarah was to make explicit the attitudes, skills, and concepts on which she based her curriculum planning, and subsequent observations and assessments. Since Victoria has no early childhood curriculum framework document, all preschool teachers in Victoria have to devise their own frameworks, but not all teachers make their assumptions as explicit as Sarah did. To help organise Sarah's thinking, Sarah and Joce together devised a simple tool (see Figure 2) that Sarah populated over a period of weeks, capturing the learning goals she chose to foster for children in the centre:

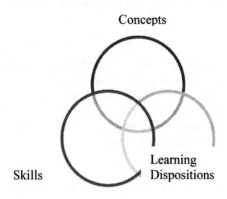

Figure 2. Template for Sarah's curriculum tool

Some initial aspects of each domain were easily identified (specific literacy and numeracy skills, for example), some were long-held underpinnings of Sarah's practice (a love of music), and some desirable goals seemed to overlap all three areas (e.g. learning how to share). For a time, development of this framework was Sarah's object. Once developed, she returned to her overall object of high quality curriculum in the centre, and reassigned the framework diagram back to the status of a tool for the centre. This was done explicitly, by reproducing the tool and displaying it in the centre for parents, other staff, and parents to see. In this way Sarah made a bold declaration of her approach to curriculum construction: 'These are the concepts, skills, and attitudes that are valued and fostered in this preschool'. Sarah also pasted a copy of the tool above her computer in her office so that, as she interpreted her observations and created assessment records, she could pay explicit attention to the areas in which children were learning and changing. Over time, Sarah can also revise the tool to accommodate important shifts in her thinking, particular educational or cultural expectations on the part of parents, and areas of learning that are highly valued by the children more than Sarah (Sarah identified gross-motor skills as one such area).

As Sarah was developing new ways of articulating her educational goals and reporting children's achievement to parents and caregivers, Lisa was trying to find a way of explaining to parents and colleagues how her commitment to socioculturally-based curriculum drove her assessment and reporting practices. During the project, Lisa seized upon an opportunity that presented itself when the school's website was being revised. Together, Lisa and Joce devised a simple pamphlet, which could be embedded in the school's website, to explain Lisa's approach. From Lisa's perspective, the pamphlet was an opportunity to clearly articulate the theoretical and philosophical basis of her program, and inform parents about the different ways they could find out about their child's progress.

From Joce's perspective, Lisa's construction of the pamphlet was interesting evidence of professional learning, since it signalled important changes in the way Lisa understood her everyday practice. At the start of the project, Lisa was already highly articulate about her practices and philosophy but she wanted to develop more sophisticated theoretical understandings. A key conceptual tool was Rogoff's (1998) three "planes" of sociocultural analysis: intrapersonal, interpersonal, and community/institutional. Having explored these planes with Joce, Lisa developed a way of thinking about reporting to parents using these analytic planes as a key conceptual tool. An excerpt from Lisa's pamphlet shows how Lisa brought the conceptual and pedagogical tools together:

> This pamphlet tells you about the principles that underpin our decisions about how to foster your child's learning and development.
>
> There are three key ideas:
>
> That children learn and develop as individuals
>
> That the learning of individual children happens through interaction with people, places, and materials; in particular, it occurs through engagement with more knowledgeable others, including their peers.
>
> That we all learn through participation in the wider communities formed through our families, across the school as a whole, and in wider society. Children contribute to these communities as well as learning from participation in the community.

The pamphlet went on to describe how parents could expect to find out about "your child's individual progress", their "learning as part of a group" and "learning as part of the community". Lisa explained that:

> Most of the learning experiences in our program occur with small groups of children.
>
> In planning for the group (either the whole group or small friendship groups) we look at what our observations of the children tell us about their relationships (who leads/follows/observes etc.), interests, knowledge and communication skills.
>
> Experiences and discussions are planned to extend the children's learning dispositions, and deepen their understanding of the world.

Most of the children in Lisa's centre continue on to the school to which her centre is attached and Lisa's analysis on Rogoff's 'community/institutional' plane of analysis emphasised this relationship:

> We are fortunate to be part of a wonderful school, one which warmly embraces the children in ECC as an important part of the community. Being part of the wider school community offers the children an opportunity to learn through modelling from older children, to develop an understanding of

the wider world (in particular the culture and experience of school in preparation for future years), to grow in confidence and knowledge through interactions with older siblings/friends.

Sarah's curriculum framework and Lisa's parent pamphlet are clear examples of how the articulation and construction of pedagogical tools can powerfully mediate teachers' professional learning. As subjects, Lisa and Sarah are entirely object-oriented in their practice: they seek to develop pedagogical ideas and artefacts that will assist them to meet their object.

What is perhaps less obvious is the way in which the development of these tools also reconstructs Sarah and Lisa as subjects. A fundamental aspect of the Vygotskian theoretical project is the effort to transcend traditional dichotomies in theories of learning, i.e. that the motive power for learning is either entirely internal (e.g. theories of maturation) or entirely external (e.g. behaviourist theories) (Rogoff, 1998). In identifying the mediating role of cultural tools, Vygotsky also showed how individuals can transcend structural limitations, through the power of their own agency, to develop themselves *from the outside*. For Lisa and Sarah, this development became a systematic, conscious process of professional learning and transformation, which continues today.

Transforming agency, transforming structures

Lisa's development of the parent pamphlet was a highly agentic act, since the resulting tool is markedly different from the mainstream (developmental) discourse of Victorian preschools. In the following section of transcript, we see the dramatic result this had at the structural level:

Lisa [I've been]… experimenting with using photos, and [concentrating] on really learning [Microsoft] Publisher and using that as a tool. Just starting to use that more as a tool to communicate with parents. So that was really exciting and then I was, I kind of got to a point where I was, okay, I want to use these more as Learning Stories. I'm going to experiment with that more, now that I'm feeling more confident with managing Publisher stuff. So I was excited about that. And then at the same time I'd written – had I written the three page summary when I'd spoke to you last?

Joce I think you were just drafting it up. Yeah.

Lisa Yeah. So that was really positive.

Joce Yeah.

Lisa To have that feedback. They basically came back and offered [dramatically improved working conditions].

Joce Wow.

Lisa They gave me … [the option of additional planning time, which would also reduce my child contact commitment by eighteen children].

Lisa's creation of the pamphlet had not only demonstrated to her Principal that she had learned how to employ up-to-date pedagogical ideas and artefacts in highly sophisticated ways, but had brought home to him the amount of work involved in constructing and enacting an effective preschool curriculum. This resulted in important structural changes in the preschool. For the record, Lisa did take up the offer of more generous non-contact time in which to further refine her plans for the development of the children, maintain relationships with parents, and continue to reflexively transform her own professional learning.

CONCLUSION

In this chapter we have argued that professional learning in early childhood settings results from the complex interplay of teacher agency and institutional structures. Furthermore, we have attempted to show how the traditional and powerful dichotomy of structure and agency can be confounded when teachers identify the contradictions resulting from this dichotomy, as they engage in day-to-day construction of centre curriculum. As Sarah learned to express the key ideas behind her centre's curriculum, and Lisa learned to make explicit links between theory and practice in a way that is accessible to parents, both teachers expressed their professional agency and challenged the persistent cultural and historical structures of early childhood services. These include rules about how children should be observed (individually), assessed (developmentally), and how parents should be informed about their children's progress (individually and with an emphasis on learning that has not yet occurred). Lisa's improved working conditions (a structural factor) resulted not just from her ability to express herself (an agentic factor) but from her developing ability to mediate and confound the structure-agency dichotomy through the development of a key pedagogical tool. Importantly, these shifts become part of a dynamic whole, shifting the context for successive opportunities for professional learning.

Overall, this chapter portrays the complex and highly contextualised nature of teachers' professional learning (McClain & Cobb, 2004; Nuttall, Doecke, Mitchell, Berry, & Illesca, 2007). Lisa's and Sarah's experiences confirm that context matters. Whilst teachers may seek professional development opportunities based on their immediate needs, these needs may be a consequence of the institutional setting and therefore difficult to address solely through the teachers' professional learning. Teachers need to be reassured that they may struggle to achieve their professional goals not because they are 'hopeless', but because Victorian preschools are not arranged in a way that easily affords the development of the teacher.

This project also seems to support the view that the learning dispositions of teachers are crucial not just in professional learning, but in curriculum construction in general. Sadler (2002, p. 50) offers an extensive list of 'desirable' teacher dispositions, including 'persistence, recovery from setbacks and failures, imagination and improvisation, experimentation, lateral thinking, confidence in tackling the unknown, self-control, infectious enthusiasm for learning, dedication to learning for mastery, joy in emerging capability, goal-directedness, palpable curiosity, and conviviality'. Sadler goes as far as to argue that "teachers' personal learning dispositions and how well teachers themselves model lifelong learning to their charges may well turn out to be key factors in how effective educational programmes can be in promoting learning dispositions in learners" (ibid.). In pursuing this idea, we have argued that learning dispositions are important because they foster teacher agency in the face of structures that can limit teachers' learning. We have also argued that agentic teachers act strategically, by developing pedagogical tools that challenging the limiting effects of institutional structures, to advance not only their learning but the learning of the children in their care.

ACKNOWLEDGEMENT

We are grateful for the receipt of a Monash University Staff Research Project Grant in 2006, which provided the funds to conduct this project.

REFERENCES

Bredekamp, S., & Copple, C. (1997). *Developmentally appropriate practice in early childhood programs* (Rev. ed.). Washington, DC: National Association for the Education of Young Children.

Carr, M., & Claxton, G. (2002). Tracking the development of learning dispositions. *Assessment in Education, 9*(1), 9–37.

Clark, C. M. (1995). *Thoughtful teaching.* New York: Teachers College Press.

Claxton, G. (1999). *Wise up: The challenge of lifelong learning.* London: Bloomsbury.

Denzin, N. K. (2001). *Interpretive interactionism* (2nd ed.). Newbury Park, CA: Sage.

Edwards, S. (2003). *'The curriculum is... ': Early childhood educators' conceptions of curriculum and developmentally appropriate practice. A comparative case study across two Victorian early childhood educational settings.* Unpublished PhD thesis, Monash University, Melbourne, Australia.

Engeström, Y. (1987). *Learning by expanding: An activity-theoretical approach to developmental research.* Helsinki: Orienta-Konsultit.

Fleer, M., & Robbins, J. (2004). 'Yeah that's what they teach you at uni, it's just rubbish': The participatory appropriation of new cultural tools as early childhood student teachers move from a developmental to a sociocultural framework for observing and planning. *Journal of Australian Research in Early Childhood Education, 11*(1), 47–62.

McClain, K., & Cobb, P. (2004). The critical role of institutional context in teacher development. In *Proceedings of the 28th conference of the international group for the psychology of mathematics education* (Vol. 3, pp. 281–288). Cape Town, South Africa: International Group for the Psychology of Mathematics Education.

Mitchell, L., & Cubey, P. (2003). *Characteristics of professional development linked to enhanced pedagogy and children's learning in early childhood settings: Best evidence synthesis.* Wellington, New Zealand: Ministry of Education.

Nuttall, J., Doecke, B., Berry, A., Illesca, B., & Mitchell, J. (2007). Fieldwork supervision: A space for professional learning. In A. Clemens, A. Berry, & A. Kostagriz (Eds.), *Dimensions of professional learning: Professionalism, practice and identity* (pp. 37–52). Rotterdam, The Netherlands: Sense Publishers.

Rogoff, B. (1998). Cognition as a collaborative process. In W. Damon (Chief Editor), D. Kuhn, & R. S. Seigler (Volume Eds.), *Cognition, perceptions and language. Handbook of child psychology* (5th ed., pp. 679–774). New York: John Wiley & Sons, Inc.

Rogoff, B. (2003). *The cultural nature of human development*. Oxford, United Kingdom: Oxford University Press.

Smith, A. B., Grima, B., Gaffney, M., Powell, K., Masse, L., & Barnett, S. (2000). *Strategic research initiative literature review: Early childhood education*. Wellington: Ministry of Education.

Sadler, R. (2002). Learning dispositions: Can we really assess them? *Assessment in Education, 9*(1), 45–51.

Joce Nuttall
Faculty of Education
Monash University
Lisa Coxon
Director
Woodleigh Early Childhood Centre
Sarah Read
Director
Parkdale Kindergarten and Preschool

JAN GEORGESON

8. THE PROFESSIONALISATION OF THE EARLY YEARS WORKFORCE

INTRODUCTION

In the United Kingdom there is a policy push towards increased professionalisation of the Early Years workforce affecting the way practitioners understand their role in working with children (Cooke & Lawton, 2008; Holland & Albon, 2006; Osgood, 2006). In this chapter I examine how this move towards professionalisation across all early years sectors came about then question how well the proposed changes to impose centrally-defined standards fit with the way many of these practitioners have been learning to do their jobs. My approach is informed by experience of working, advising, and inspecting in early years settings, from assessing candidates for the new professional status, and by my research in settings from the Private and Voluntary Sector (PVS).

I have adopted a sociocultural perspective and have found it helpful to think about each setting as a system of purposeful activity, drawing on concepts developed in Activity Theory (Engeström, 1999). Edwards has argued that development of early education practice needs "to be seen not only in terms of curriculum, but also in terms of a classroom or preschool setting as an *activity system* in which particular ways of being and thinking are supported (Edwards, 2004, p. 89, my emphasis). This has led to my understanding of the resources and routines of nursery practice as culturally–honed tools or artefacts, which help to guide practitioners into ways of working that fit their particular setting. These resources include the particular ways of speaking adopted in different settings, and I shall present evidence from research that describes local interactional microclimates in preschool settings. My findings have prompted me to question whether the imposition of a top-down strategy of professional standardization runs the risk of losing good local practice attuned to local communities, and threatens to turn participation in meaningful activity into performance of borrowed 'best practice'.

PROFESSIONALISATION AND CREDENTIALISATION

Over the last ten years, the move towards professionalisation has been accompanied by an increasing range of routes for practitioners to upgrade their qualifications through further study. These include foundation degrees and new broadly based courses in early childhood studies (Nurse, 2007). However, recent proposals have

S. Edwards, J. Nuttall (eds.), Professional Learning in Early Childhood Settings, 115–130.

introduced a new strategy to bring about improvements in the workforce, which will entail a different approach to professional learning. As part of the Children's Workforce Strategy, 'experts' will be placed in all early years settings to promote the government's 'transformational reform agenda designed to improve life chances for all and reduce inequalities in our society' (Department for Education and Skills [DfES], 2006).

This strategy has necessitated the creation of a new government agency, the Children's Workforce Development Council (CWDC), to promote an appropriate infrastructure so that 'that the people working with children have the best possible training, qualifications, support and advice'. The CWDC aims to achieve the goal of a graduate-level practitioner in each early years setting by 2015. These high status individuals will improve practice by acting as 'agents for change', which they will bring about by providing role models for less well-qualified staff, by influencing policy, by communicating good Early Years practice effectively to parents and carers, and by maintaining strong links with other agencies (CWDC, 2008). Specifically, the strategy involves the introduction of a new Early Years Practitioner Status (EYPS), which is not a new qualification *per se* but a 'status' akin to Qualified Teacher Status (QTS). Once this has been achieved, the new EYPs' influence will be maintained by further input from CWDC-commissioned training packages.

The presence of EYPs in Early Years settings is intended to improve practice informally, rather than through the provision of formal courses or training opportunities. Knight (2002), analysing recent changes to professional development, argues for a new conceptualisation which:

> Shifts the emphasis in professional development thinking away from individuals and courses to systemic, complex understandings of the ways in which learning is created and shared within communities of practice. ..[..] the heart of professional development is good, everyday practice that purposefully keeps improving itself through fresh problem-working. [....]. Knowing created in one place does not easily transfer, in the form of knowledge, to another (Knight, 2002, p. 229).

Knight (ibid) argues that paying attention to who is leading practice within a setting is one way to ensure that 'everyone is touched by continuing professional development activity because it pervades daily practice'. To achieve this, the person who is leading practice needs to be capable of 'leading to learn' and EYPs are to take on this role of leadership for learning within Early Years settings.

PRESENT-DAY PRESCHOOL PROVISION IN THE UK

To understand why the EYPS as a model of professional development might not sit comfortably in some Early Years sectors in the UK, requires some awareness of current preschool provision and how it got to be that way. Many commentators on provision for early childhood education and care in the UK have concluded that it is at best diverse or at worst 'disparate and disorganised' (Vincent & Ball, 2001).

Before they reach the age of statutory schooling at five, children might attend private, workplace or local authority day nurseries, sessional community groups run by the voluntary sector, state maintained nursery schools or reception classes, private independent pre-preparatory schools or classes, childminders, or indeed some mixture of these settings. These different kinds of provision might take place in village or church halls, private homes, purpose-built Children's Centres, or traditional school buildings. The different settings have different origins, having developed in response to different local contingencies in the past, are financed through different and ever-changing funding streams, and accommodate the different needs or preferences of the families who live or work nearby.

Against this background of diversity of structure and function, all settings receiving government funding have been subjected to a unified inspection regime and a common educational framework since the introduction of free preschool places in England between 1996 and 2004. All children aged three and over are now entitled to government funding for some form of preschool education, and working towards the same early learning goals (Qualifications and Curriculum Authority, 2000), by attending one or more the wide variety of settings outlined above. The curriculum frameworks for birth to three and three to the end of the school-year-in-which-children-become-five were amalgamated into the Early Years Foundation Stage in 2008, thereby completing the unification of guidelines for how and what young children should learn before they embark on Year 1 of formal schooling.

This standardisation of curriculum guidelines for three- and four-year-olds began at a time when tensions were already developing in the early years sector. Changes to education in the UK in the 1980s and 1990s affecting the educational climate in general were gradually exerting downward pressure on the preschool sector. The advent of the National Curriculum in 1988 and the expansion of the remit of the inspection service in 1993 were cornerstones of a government agenda to take control of content and delivery of education in the statutory sector, and had a profound influence on teachers who worked there. Changes came thick and fast and teachers' adherence to the new regimes was scrutinised at every point. New legislation which affected the preschool sector at this time was perhaps better received; for example, the Children Act (DfES, 1989) was, on the whole, seen as beneficial and in children's interests. At the same time, however, the introduction of Standard Assessment Tasks (SATs) and league tables to primary schools exerted subtle pressures on some facets of the preschool sector, as staff began to feel the need to advance preschool children along the path to achieving the government's benchmarks at the end of Key Stage One of the primary phase.

This sequence of legislative changes affected not only what teachers were expected to do, but altered the whole climate to one of performativity (Ball, 2001). The onslaught of initiatives and constant changes in the legislative framework introduced feelings of fear and uncertainty, as teachers strove to keep up with what they were supposed to be doing, while being assessed against ever-changing criteria. Teaching entailed a new way of being from the pre-National Curriculum days, when teachers had been able to rely on their own professionalism as the arbiter of what was appropriate for them to be doing. Increasingly, it seemed as if the traditional ethos of professionalism was no longer trusted to deliver what was required (Hanlon, 1998, p. 52).

It was against this background of uncertainty and fear of judgement in the maintained (i.e. government-funded) sector, that government funding for preschool education in the form of the nursery voucher scheme was introduced in 1996. This signalled the spread of accountability and standardisation into preschool provision. The government needed to ensure that places in the non-maintained sector could be viewed as offering something equivalent to the provision in maintained nursery classes and schools, as part of the need to give a 'veneer of comparability' (Penn, 2000, p. 2) with state and independent educational provision.

The educational provision in all settings receiving the grant was therefore inspected to the same standards, using the same inspection framework. Although considerations arising from other government agendas, such as inclusion for children with special educational needs or at risk of social exclusion, were promoting diversity, the climate of accountability pushed towards homogeneity. In the preschool sector, where provision was so very diverse because of its history and differing functions, it was particularly difficult to balance the need to be accountable for reaching centrally defined standards with meeting the needs of the particular community served.

The commodification of the preschool sector had already started with the expansion of private day-care in the 1980s and the growth of businesses running chains of nurseries. Voluntary providers were then also drawn into the realities of competition, scrutiny and what Ball (2001) describes as "fabrication" (p. 148), lured on by what represented, for their meagre budgets, lucrative governmental funding – a case of cash for accountability. This new ethos ran counter to the spirit of community service in which playgroups had been established. Additional stresses were caused when the balance between supply and demand for preschool places was upset by the introduction of 'voucher money'. Many parents opted to send their four-year-olds to school rather than to non-maintained provision, prompted by concerns to secure a school place for their child on reaching statutory school age (Anning & Edwards, 1999, p. 9). This trend has continued and may since have been exacerbated by the advent of the Sure Start initiative (Barnes, et al., 2007). Playgroup numbers fell; some settings were forced to close and the spectre of closure hung over the rest of the voluntary sector. The introduction of nursery vouchers heralded a succession of government initiatives and legislation that "plunged Early Childhood Education into changes in practice at a pace and depth never before experienced" (Nutbrown, 2002, p. 2). The combination of these uncertainties presented a serious challenge to the confidence and commitment of PVS practitioners, many of whom were working for love rather than money, and to whom the sudden need to be accountable and to meet rigidly defined standards came as a deep shock.

PROFESSIONAL LEARNING PATHWAYS IN THE EARLY YEARS SECTOR

The diversity of provision for early childhood education in the UK is matched by the diversity of qualifications held by the practitioners who work there, and this is associated with the many different routes practitioners can take into working with young children. Qualifications range from degrees and postgraduate certificates, through various vocational qualifications, with some practitioners having no formal qualifications at all.

Classes, units, and schools in the state sector are staffed by teachers who will, for the most part, have followed the traditional path towards professional status by learning their professional knowledge before they practice (Nurse, 2007). Some of the older members of the profession might have trained via three-year Certificate of Education courses in a teacher training college, but most teachers now achieve QTS by following a BEd degree course or taking a one-year postgraduate course after completing their degree. As well as qualified teachers, early years provision in the state sector also employs practitioners without QTS, but with other specified qualifications, who carry out an increasingly wide range of learning support functions.

In preschool settings in the private and voluntary sector, where opportunities for training have in the past been limited, practitioners have learnt to do their jobs gradually as they moved from novice to experienced worker, through various forms of legitimate peripheral participation in communities of practice (Lave & Wenger, 1991). In Lave and Wenger's (1991) words, learning to participate is not "merely a condition for membership, but is itself an evolving form of membership" (p.53). In playgroups, mothers might start as volunteer helpers and progress to the role of trained staff, often when their own children leave to attend school. In day nurseries, young girls (and it is mainly girls) start their training under the guidance of more experienced colleagues. If they are following the National Vocational Qualification (NVQ) route their training will be competency-based and often assessed by in-house NVQ assessors. It is easy to see how the practice of those working in such settings can be deeply influenced by what has happened there in the past and by the people currently in post, most of whom tend to be drawn from the local community.

In addition to any formal training, practitioners in private and voluntary sector settings come to know how to do their jobs as they learn how to work with the resources which they encounter their setting. Taking a broad view of such resources, this includes everything that a setting uses or produces, including both tangible objects (such as source books, toys, books, materials, plans, letters and pieces of work) as well as unwritten routines and procedures (such as break-times and registration). In Vygotskian terms, these are the tools or artefacts that mediate practitioners' response to the task which society has entrusted to them. Such artefacts are 'products of human history' (Cole, 1996, p. 118), a valuable source of crystallised wisdom.

PRACTITIONER LEARNING AND THE 'NURSERY TREASURE CHEST'

Preschool settings select tools or artefacts from this 'nursery treasure chest' of items and activities that have been accumulating over the years, sometimes recommended by educational theorists, sometimes developed by gifted practitioners. The English introduction to Froebel's innovatory approach to nursery education, for example, focuses on the "seven gifts" (Ronge & Ronge, 1884). The nursery treasure chest includes objects that afford particular kinds of behaviour and children can learn about these affordances by playing with these objects. These affordances can be physical (Gibson, 1979; Lockman, 2000), or social, in that they afford interaction (for example, see-saw games), or cultural, that is, objects and activities which lead children into learning about their own and other cultures (Evaldsson & Corsaro, 1998; Kane & Furth, 1993; Lobman, 2003). Children learn to use these tools or take part in these activities under the guidance of more experienced users, including other children (Hedegaard, 2002; Rogoff, 1990).

The nursery treasure chest provides practitioners with a bank of objects and practices that have proved useful, popular, or successful in appealing to children in the past, and are available for use, in the same or different ways, by the present group. The contents of the nursery treasure chest, both physical and mental, have been honed by generations of skilled users and, by providing children with access to these treasures, preschool practitioners can benefit from this accumulated wisdom without necessarily engaging directly with the theory that lies behind their original use. Although some researchers have voiced concern that the policy initiatives of the 1990s were accompanied by a "denial of the history of early childhood education" (Nutbrown, 2002, p. 4), the continued use of the objects and activities in the nursery treasure chest ensures that the past continues to influence practice today.

PRACTITIONER LEARNING IN CONTEXT

Practitioners' use of the ubiquitous nursery treasure chest in any preschool setting is learned through everyday practice, informed by observations of, and interactions with, other people in the setting. However, while the nursery treasure chest provides the basic diet (to mix metaphors) for a whole range of settings, the way in which it is used in any particular setting gives it its own distinctive flavour. Thinking of early years settings as activity systems encourages consideration of ways in which practitioners' use of tools and artefacts has been shaped by both the history and current demands of that group, how it will be influenced by what is currently happening in the community, and by implicit and explicit constraints on their continued use.

The introduction of the unified inspection regime can be seen as the introduction of new rules and constraints into preschool practice as well as the instigation of changes in the communities in which the settings were situated. It also led to subtle changes in the object of the settings' activity. It meant that, for the first time, many settings which had previously existed mainly to offer play opportunities or care were suddenly accountable for the provision of educational opportunities, if they wanted to benefit from government funding. Settings in the private and voluntary sector needed to consider what they offered in the context of other local provision, as the introduction of publicly available inspection reports suddenly made possible the sort of comparisons between settings that were never considered before. Practitioners also became accountable for their use of resources and activities; inspection meant that they had to examine the reasons behind what they had before done instinctively, or from an unspoken agreement that this was 'a good thing'. This in itself might have offered opportunities to make explicit many taken-for-granted practices, although Knight argues that the value of reflection on practice has been overplayed (Knight, 2002). Either way, the wider context in which this re-evaluation of practice was occurring was not conducive to calm reflection, or even continued confidence in the tools through which had learnt to do their jobs.

Practitioners were fearful and suspicious of the new inspection regime, uncertain about what it was that they were expected to do and how this fitted in with what parents, or teachers in schools, were doing. It disrupted practitioners' understanding of their role and of the object of their activity. Practitioners who had years of experience of successfully providing care and education for pre-school children in their community lost confidence in what they were doing and relied increasingly on official sources like the QCA document (Qualifications and Curriculum Authority, 2000) or support from teacher-mentors to see them through inspections. They borrowed tools from school practice, such as worksheets and flash cards, to make their provision seem more 'educational' but these borrowings were not underpinned by the same kind of knowledge-in-practice which had supported their use of playdough or domestic play resources.

THE CALL FOR IMPROVEMENT IN THE QUALITY OF THE EARLY YEARS
WORKFORCE

In 1996, during the early stages of this upheaval, a national longitudinal study of children attending different kinds of preschool provision began. the *Effective Provision of Pre-school Education* (EPPE) project. This study adopted a School Effectiveness Research (SER) design and is described on the project website as:

> The first major study in the United Kingdom to focus specifically on the effectiveness of early years education. The EPPE project is a large scale, longitudinal study of the progress and development of 3,000 children in various types of pre-school education. ...[..].. It will help to identify the aspects of pre-school provision which have a positive impact on children's attainment, progress and development, and so provide guidance on good practice (EPPE Project website, 2008).

The project team collected a range of measurable data using environmental rating scales, based on ECERS-R (Harms & Clifford, 1998), and a variety of scales and questionnaires to compile demographic data. They then carried out multilevel modelling to tease out the statistical effects of preschool provision over and above the effects of factors such as child health, gender, and family background

(Sammons, et al., 2002). This large-scale project has yielded a substantial body of findings about the positive effects of preschool education and the quality of the home learning environment. The project team has also made comparisons between types of settings:

> There are significant differences between individual pre-school settings and their impact on children; some settings are more effective than others in promoting positive child outcomes. .. Good quality can be found across all types of early years settings; however quality was higher overall in settings integrating care and education and in nursery schools (Sylva, Melhuish, Sammons, Siraj-Blatchford, & Taggart, 2003).

These results echo findings from government inspections over a similar time period in which playgroups and day nurseries performed less well than other forms of provision, in a comparison of inspection results (Tomlinson, 2000).

Findings from the EPPE project have become well known for their contribution to 'evidence based policy' in early years education and care (Siraj-Blatchford, Taggart, Sylva, Sammons, & Melhuish, 2008; Sylva et al., 2004). However, the way in which these results have sometimes been interpreted has added to the impression that something needed to be done about the quality of staff in preschool settings in the private and voluntary sectors. In particular, reports from EPPE drew attention to the association between effectiveness of settings and the level of training of managers, which the project team use to support calls for more highly trained managers (preferably teachers) in preschool settings (Sylva, Sammons, Siraj-Blatchford, Melhuish, & Quinn, 2001, p. 11). For example, the following is an extract from a submission by EPPE to the Department of Work and Pensions in 2003:

> *EPPE also shows that centre managers' qualification levels are related to quality, with centres where managers were at level 5 (i.e. teaching qualifications) had higher scores on quality profiles.* The multilevel analyses indicate that a higher level of staff qualifications (i.e. % of staff at trained teacher level 5) is associated with better outcomes for several social behavioural measures and also for pre-reading progress. These results have implications for policymakers and practitioners and suggest that promoting the quality of all types of provision (but especially those which our profiles suggest are weaker) will benefit young children from every social class and lead to better outcomes by the start of primary school (Sylva, et al. 2003: italics added).

The finding I have highlighted here – that high quality settings are associated with highly qualified staff – is widely quoted and has had a strong influence on policy. While there could be several explanations for this (such as that highly-qualified staff being more likely to seek out, and be appointed to, positions in those well-resourced settings that also tend to accrue higher scores on environmental rating scales) this finding is often interpreted as evidence of a causal link between positive child outcomes and the presence of staff with graduate level qualifications.

For example, in an article for the *Guardian* newspaper, the team leader for a group of Children's Centre teachers is reported explaining the role of teachers in nurseries: "An important study known as EPPE demonstrated that teachers bring benefits to a birth-to-five setting that nursery staff alone can't" (Tickle, 2006). A year later, the New Vision Group of educationalists, discussing EPPE's findings, referred to, "The private and voluntary sector, where low levels of funding lead to low-quality and poorly paid staff. Few of these have QTS" (New Vision Group, 2007, p. 3). This repeated assumption, of a causal link between highly-qualified staff and good child outcomes, serves to undermine the worth of other less well-qualified (but often highly-experienced) staff – positioned as low-quality – and privilege those with graduate status.

Evidence from EPPE fed into a national consultation in the summer of 2005 on the future of the children's workforce. The government's response to this consultation was to draw up a transformational reform agenda with a clear mission to change the early years workforce (DfES, 2006). On the Children's Workforce Development Council website there is further evidence of over-interpretation of EPPE's findings to support the drive towards professionalisation:

> Evidence from the Effective Provision of Pre-School Education (EPPE) study shows that improving the quality of the early years experience is directly related to better outcomes for children (CWDC, 2008).

This suggests that EPPE carried out some kind of intervention in which they improved the quality of settings and that this led to better outcomes, whereas no such intervention took place; EPPE's findings are based on statistical analyses following one cohort of children through preschool years and on into school.

The CWDC's new strategy centres round a simple message; "Our vision is for a graduate-led early years workforce delivering a high quality Early Years Foundation Stage to improve outcomes for children" (CWDC, 2008). This has clearly set out a top-down strategy to improve the EY workforce by the introduction of practitioners, educated to graduate level, who meet and maintain a set of standards drawn up by the CWDC. It remains to be seen how this distillation of the complexity of EPPE's findings into a simple cause-and-effect model – that graduates cause better child outcomes – will play out. Currently "graduates with a non-relevant degree and little or no experience of work with young children [...] or those with completely unrelated degrees wanting a career change and with a desire to understand and work with young children" (University of Nottingham, 2008), can train for free for 12 months, be assessed to see whether they demonstrate in written tasks and interview that they meet the standards for EYPS and are then deemed ready to be leading practice. This follows the logic of the cause and effect model; graduate practitioners will be in place therefore child outcomes will now improve. Interestingly, although there is some recognition that these individuals should have had some experience with young children, the barriers to achieving EYPS are concerned with level of qualification, not level of experience.

LEARNING HOW TO INTERACT IN PEDAGOGICAL EXCHANGES

There is one feature of 'effective' provision that has emerged from the case studies that accompanied the EPPE project which the project team have identified as particularly important in promoting children's development and which is increasingly mentioned in the context of professional development, including the standards for EYPS. This is 'sustained shared thinking' between adults and children (Sylva et al., 2004). EYPs are expected to lead practice to promote sustained shared thinking between staff and children in their settings; however, my own research suggests that there are subtle but important differences between the interactional microclimates in settings that support sustained shared thinking, and that such differences are born out of the particular ways in which individual settings have developed to carry out the activity of preschool provision in their particular community. This has implications for how practitioners learn to engage children in sustained shared thinking and, in particular, how practitioners with EPYS fit into this learning process.

My research (Georgeson, 2006) investigated practitioners', parents' and children's understanding or awareness of the culture of their preschool setting in four preschool settings from the private and voluntary sectors in the West Midlands. In the following section, I shall use findings from case studies of these settings to illustrate differences in interactive style that can affect how children and adults talk. The settings differed in their organisational structure and pedagogical subculture and these differences are summarised in Table 1:

Table 1. Summary of the four settings in the West Midlands project.

Name of setting*	Setting type	Organisational style	Pedagogical emphasis
Village Hall	Community Preschool	Organic, open, egalitarian structure, weak boundaries between home and preschool	Setting prioritises socialization for children before they start school.
Rocking Horse	Private Day Nursery	-Hierarchical staffing structure but blurred boundaries between home and nursery	Setting prioritises socialization in homely surroundings.
Orchard House	Private Nursery School offering full day care	Very hierarchical staffing structure and clear boundaries between home and nursery	High educational emphasis in school-like atmosphere
Building Blocks	Community Preschool within charitable organisation	Complex organisational structure, blurred boundaries between home and preschool	High educational emphasis aimed at both children and families

*Not real names

Four case studies were built up from observation, documentary analysis, and structured interviews. The perspectives of staff were elicited during career biography interviews, and parents' views on preschool provision were sought through questionnaires. These findings are reported in full elsewhere (Georgeson, 2006), and showed that both parents and staff had awareness and approval of their own setting's particular organisational style and pedagogical emphasis, and that these differences in ethos were apparent in the style of interaction in that setting. This was evident in the third part of the project in which children aged three and four were encouraged to talk about preschool activities as they looked at photographs of their own and the other settings in the project. Fine-grained linguistic analysis based on concepts derived from Systemic Functional Linguistics, in particular the work of Painter (1999), provided insights into the particular interactional style of individual settings. The differences in children's interactional style were then related to differences in organisational style and pedagogical emphasis, and to observational data about the ways in which adults spoke in the differing settings.

The findings revealed subtle but potentially influential ways in which interactional style differed between settings, of which staff would need to be aware when they engaged children in sustained shared thinking. For example, the greatest proportion of instances of co-construction was found at Rocking Horse, the homely day nursery. This is consistent with findings from the case study, which had revealed an ethos of social awareness and pragmatic consideration of the needs of other people. The children at Rocking Horse also used more connecting elements ('and', 'as well'), repetition, and extension to link what they wanted to say with what has been said before, while the children at Orchard House (the school-like day nursery) presented their own opinions in opposition to the previous utterances. This was mirrored in the way adults were observed to speak to children, with Rocking Horse staff frequently linking their utterances to children's own experiences both at home and at nursery, while Orchard House staff tended to bring in new information, often from their own experience, or provide new knowledge.

The weaving together of one's own and another's thoughts, which is required in co-construction, could be seen as requiring a different kind of understanding of two points of view, in contrast with the 'that's wrong; this is right' rhetoric which characterised the countering exchanges at Orchard House. Painter draws attention to the importance for children's cognitive development of becoming aware of other people's ideas and integrating these with one's own thoughts: "The ability to represent the cognitions of oneself and others can be seen as fundamental, not only for monitoring one's own learning, but for reflecting on the world of ideas and beliefs in general" (Painter, 1999, p. 320).

It seems possible that children and staff at Rocking Horse, in their tendency to build on the comments and experiences of other people, were developing a style of thinking that would equip children well for learning through contact with other people's ideas. Children at Orchard House, on the other hand, were learning that pedagogic exchanges were about displaying your knowledge to your audience.

Children at Rocking Horse also used different verbal strategies to offer information; they tended to objectise uncertainty by using words like 'maybe' or 'it might' while Orchard House children subjectised their assertions with 'I bet' or 'I think'. Analysis of fragments of adult talk from observations revealed a similar pattern; staff at Rocking Horse tended to be more tentative, softening the way they corrected children's mistakes by using 'maybe', or putting an alternative interpretation forward prefaced by 'it might be'. These features were mirrored in children's talk; children were learning from staff how to put forward an alternative opinion without offending anyone. This was in contrast to staff at Orchard House who explicitly sought children's individual opinions and praised children who came up with the right answer. Children responded to this by staking their claims to knowledge with 'I think' or 'I bet'.

Other features of interactional styles emerged from the other settings, notably a differential use of personal pronouns in Building Blocks, which was the setting with the highest proportion of children who were learning English in addition to their home language. In this setting children hardly ever used the first person plural ('we', 'us', 'our') but used second person grammatical forms ('you', 'your') far more frequently. To an unfamiliar ear, this had the effect of making children's talk seem rather intrusive, and occasionally accusatory. Adult talk here appeared somewhat stark in comparison with other settings, with more direct instructions and more guidance given to individual children (and so plenty of second person forms). In the context of children learning English as an additional language, these linguistic strategies were highly adaptive, and much clearer than the first person plural conventions of teacherese ('Susan! We never bite our friends') or oblique references instead of direct instruction ('I'm waiting till everyone's quiet'/'someone's not listening' versus 'Please stop talking now so you can listen to me').

THE INTERFACE BETWEEN EYPS AND LOCAL INTERACTIONAL STYLES

These subtle differences in interactional style provided an induction into the language of pedagogic exchanges that was finely tuned to suit particular children from particular communities. This has implications for how early years practitioners can help all children, including those who might find transition difficult, to settle into preschool provision and to prepare them for the move into statutory provision. This amounts to what Painter describes as 'semiotic preparation for schooling', an orientation to how meanings are made and shared in learning contexts (Painter, 1999). However, these are not aspects of practice that lend themselves readily to training; instead they form part of the particular ways of being, doing and saying which practitioners learn through participation in an activity, and which go on to provide them with moment-on-moment knowledge about how to behave and respond in the different contexts in which they operate.

The significance of subtle variations of interactional style in early years settings has long been recognised; researchers such as Brice Heath and Lubeck have demonstrated that parents and practitioners from different communities have their own ways of interacting with children which are born out of the values and attitudes which shape their lives (Brice Heath, 1983; Lubeck, 1985). The work of Brice Heath also demonstrates how difficult it can be for children whose home style of interacting differs markedly from that of mainstream schooling. If preschool provision is to provide a bridge for children to help them move from home environment to school environment – to provide semiotic preparation for schooling – then preschool practitioners need to be able to talk to children in ways which will be familiar to them and help them to understand what is expected of them in a pedagogic exchange. However, much of what contributes to making talk in settings special can be difficult to verbalise and therefore difficult to share explicitly. My research suggests that there are aspects of practice, like use of pronouns, which are unlikely to form the focus of staff discussions but which nonetheless contribute to what it is about a setting that makes it unique, and allow it to occupy its particular socio-ecological niche.

How the introduction of experts like EYPs might contribute to this process would seem to depend on who these experts are, how well they understand the communities where they work, and how good they are at 'leading from within'. The elevation of one member of staff to the level of expert runs counter to the more collaborative ways in which many practitioners from the private and (especially) the voluntary sector have learned how to do their jobs. The first wave of EYPs were mainly experienced staff who were already able to meet the qualification criteria and who saw EYPS as a useful addition to their CV, possibly with an eye to the future when all settings would need an EYP in post. Many held senior positions in their settings or organisations, but had worked their way from the edges of practice to the centre, changing practice in the process, as they worked alongside their colleagues. It could be expected that 'experts' or 'agents for change' like these would be able to contribute positively to the professional learning of others, as long as they retained their confidence in the embodied knowledge of their colleagues about how to respond to local contingencies.

But what about those graduates who have acquired their knowledge of early years through much less direct experience of working with children? Having learnt about child development, policy, and practice through a year of full-time study and placement, they are set to act as agents for change in settings anxious to appoint staff with EYPS. When teachers are trained in this way (through the acquisition of professional knowledge before practice), they have an explicit probationary period when they are supported in learning their job and then gradually work their way into more senior positions. They are not expected to go in and lead and change practice in schools straightaway.

Much of the success of this policy will depend on which aspects of practice the newly recognised EYPs see as needing to be changed. In their training, and in subsequent CWDC-approved programmes of support, they are introduced to what is considered 'best practice' in early years provision. This commodification of practice is fraught with danger, particularly in the context of working with practitioners who might lack confidence in their ability to meet the requirements of educational provision. When challenged, non-EYPS practitioners might not be able to articulate why they are doing things the way they do, reminding them they do not have EYPS and are not the 'experts'. This may influence them to place less trust in their own experienced-based knowledge about how to care for and interact with children in their settings.

The attitude of non-EYPS practitioners to the artefacts that mediate the activity in their settings might also change. The unquestioned adoption of 'best practice' from outside the setting could affect the subtleties of interaction and operation that have evolved over time to meet the particular needs of the community the setting serves. Bits of equipment and practice from curriculum guidelines and training vignettes can acquire almost fetishistic properties and then be brought out for special 'displays of quality' (Ball, 2001, p. 210) to impress inspectors and prospective parents. These practices will not necessarily fit into practitioners' understanding of how they enact preschool provision in their setting, understandings which have been carefully built up as they have taken part in the everyday life of the settings. Practice then becomes performance, rather than the participation in activity grounded in the history and culture of individual settings.

There is increasing recognition of the need for more effective links between settings, families and the local communities, and "a growing body of literature which questions traditional notions of professionalism, notions which distance professionals from those they serve and prioritise one group's knowledge over another's" (Oberhuemer, 2005, p. 13). The elevation of some practitioners with graduate qualifications to the role of 'agents for change' runs the risk of losing the instinctive and implicit expertise of those practitioners who, for a variety of reasons, might find it difficult to follow the path towards graduate status. These are often the practitioners who are closest to their local communities and, if the new workforce strategy really is to be "driven by local decisions in response to local needs" (DfES, 2006), their experience and understanding must also be incorporated into this process through consultation and collaboration.

REFERENCES

Anning, A., & Edwards, A. (1999). *Promoting children's learning from birth to five*. Buckingham: Open University Press.

Ball, S. (2001). Performatives and fabrications in the education economy. In D. Gleeson & C. Husbands (Eds.), *The performing school: Managing, teaching and learning in a performance culture* (pp. 210–226). London: Routledge Falmer.

Barnes, J., Cheng, H., Frost, M., Harper, G., Howden, B., Lattin-Rawstrone, R., et al. (2007, June). *Changes in the characteristics of sure start local programme areas in rounds 1 to 4 between 2000/2001 and 2004/2005*. London: DCSF, Sure Start Report Number 21. Retrieved October 28, 2008, from http://www.surestart.gov.uk/publications/?Document=1908

Brice Heath, S. (1983). *Ways with words: Language, life and work in communities and classrooms*. Cambridge: Cambridge University Press.

Cole, M. (1996). *Cultural psychology*. Cambridge, MA: Harvard University Press.

Cooke, G., & Lawton, K. (2008). *For love or money: Pay, progression and professionalisation in the 'early years' workforce*. London: IPPR.

Children's Workforce Development Council. (2008). *I am a very experienced practitioner at Level 3 - whey do I need a degree to be awarded EYPS?* Retrieved October 28, 2008, from http://www.cwdcouncil.org.uk/about/faq#Q_432

Children's Workforce Development Council. (2008). *Welcome to early years.* Retrieved August 20, 2008, from http://www.cwdcouncil.org.uk/early-years

Department for Education and Skills. (1989). *The children act.* London: HMSO.

Department for Education and Skills. (2006). *Children's workforce strategy; Building a world-class workforce for children, young people and families.* Retrieved April 20, 2008, from http://www.everychildmatters.gov.uk/resources-and-practice/IG00038/

Edwards, A. (2004). Understanding context, understanding practice in early education. *European Early Childhood Education Research Journal, 12*, 85–101.

Engeström, Y. (1999). Activity theory and individual and social transformations. In Y. Engestrom, R. Miettinen, & R.-L. Punamaki (Eds.), *Perspectives on activity theory.* Cambridge: Cambridge University Press.

Effective Provision of Pre-school Education Project. (2008). *EPPE 1997–2003: Introduction.* Retrieved April 20, 2008, from http://www.ioe.ac.uk/schools/ecpe/eppe/eppe/eppeintro.htm

Evaldsson, A., & Corsaro, W. (1998). Play and games in the peer cultures of preschool and preadolescent children: An interpretative approach. *Childhood, 5*, 377–402.

Georgeson, J. (2006). *Differences in preschool culture: Organisation, pedagogy and interaction in four selected settings.* University of Birmingham.

Gibson, J. J. (1979). *The ecological approach to visual perception.* Boston: Houghton Mifflin.

Hanlon, G. (1998). Professionalism as enterprise. *Sociology, 32*, 43–63.

Harms, T., & Clifford, R. (1998). *Early childhood environment rating scale* (Rev. Ed.). New York: Teachers College Press.

Hedegaard, M. (2002). *Learning and child development.* Aarhus: Aarhus University Press.

Holland, P., & Albon, D. (2006, September). *'I'm now seen as a professional': Multiple perceptions of the professional role within the early years workforc'.* Paper presented at the EECERA 16th annual conference 'Democracy and Culture in Early Childhood Education', Reyjkavik, Iceland.

Kane, S., & Furth, H. (1993). Children constructing social reality: A frame analysis of social pretend play. *Human Development, 36*, 199–214.

Knight, P. (2002). A systemic approach to professional development. *Teaching and Teacher Education, 18*(3), 229–241.

Lave, J., & Wenger, E. (1991). *Situated learning: Legitimate peripheral participation.* Cambridge: Cambridge University Press.

Lobman, C. L. (2003). What should we create today? Improvisational teaching in play-based classrooms. *Early Years, 23*, 131–142.

Lockman, J. J. (2000). A perception-action perspective on tool use development. *Child Development, 71*, 137–144.

Lubeck, S. (1985). *Sandbox society: Early education in black and white America - a comparative ethnography.* London: Falmer Press.

New Vision Group. (2007, July 10). Do you have the vision and the courage, Prime Minister? *The Guardian*, p. 3.

Nurse, A. D. (Ed.). (2007). *The new early years professional.* Abingdon: Routledge.

Nutbrown, C. (2002). Early childhood education in contexts of change. In C. Nutbrown (Ed.), *Research studies in early childhood education* (pp. 1–9). Stoke on Trent: Trentham Books.

Oberhuemer, P. (2005). Conceptualising the early childhood pedagogue: Policy approaches and issues of professionalism. *European Early Childhood Research Journal, 13*, 5–16.

Osgood, J. (2006). Deconstructing professionalism in early years childhood education: Resisting the regulatory gaze. *Contemporary Issues in Early Childhood, 7*(1), 5–14.

Painter, C. (1999). *Learning through language in early childhood.* London: Cassell.

Penn, H. (2000). *Early childhood services: Theory, policy and practice.* Buckingham: Open University Press.

Qualifications and Curriculum Authority. (2000). *Curriculum guidance for the foundation stage.* London: Qualifications and Curriculum Authority/DfEE.

Rogoff, B. (1990). *Apprenticeship in thinking: Cognitive development in social context*. New York: Oxford University Press.

Ronge, J., & Ronge, B. (1884). A practical guide to the English kindergarten. In *Evolution of English nursery education* (Vol. VI, pp. 3–167). London: Routledge.

Sammons, P., Sylva, K., Melhuish, E., Siraj-Blatchford, I., Taggart, B., & Elliot, K. (2002). *Technical paper 8a: Measuring the impact of pre-school on children's cognitive progress over the pre-school period*. London: Institute of Education, University of London.

Siraj-Blatchford, I., Taggart, B., Sylva, K., Sammons, P., & Melhuish, E. (2008). Towards the transformation of practice in early childhood education: The effective provision of pre-school education (EPPE) project. *Cambridge Journal of Education, 38*(1), 23–63.

Sylva, K., Melhuish, E. C., Sammons, P., Siraj-Blatchford, I., & Taggart, B. (2003). Appendix 13, Memorandum submitted by the Effective Provision of Pre-School Education Project (EPPE) (CC 17). Select Committee on Work and Pensions Written Evidence. UK Parliament. 12 February. Retrieved October 28, 2008, from http://www.publications.parliament.uk/pa/cm200203/cmselect/cmworpen/564/564we14.htm

Sylva, K., Melhuish, E. C., Sammons, P., Siraj-Blatchford, I., & Taggart, B. (2004). *The effective provision of pre-School education (EPPE) project: Technical paper 12 - the final report*. London: Institute of Education, University of London.

Sylva, K., Sammons, P., Siraj-Blatchford, I., Melhuish, E., & Quinn, L. (2001, September). *The effective provision of pre-school education (EPPE) project: A longitudinal study funded by the DFES (1997–2003)*. Paper presented at the British Educational Research Association (BERA) annual conference. 13th–15th September, Leeds University, UK.

Tickle, L. (2006, June 6). Teacher goes to nursery. *The Guardian*. Retrieved October 28, 2008, from http://www.guardian.co.uk/education/2006/jun/06/schools.earlyyearseducation

Tomlinson, M. (2000). *The quality of nursery education for three- and four-year-olds 1999–2000*. London: Office for Standards in Education.

University of Nottingham. (2008). *Early Years Professional Status (EYPS)*. Retrieved 20 August 2008, from http://www.nene.ac.uk/courses/undergraduate/detail/?id=0291

Vincent, C., & Ball, S. J. (2001). A market in love? Choosing pre-school childcare. *British Educational Research Journal, 27*, 633–651.

Jan Georgeson
Department of Education,
University of Oxford

JOCE NUTTALL AND SUSAN EDWARDS

9. FUTURE DIRECTIONS IN RESEARCHING PROFESSIONAL LEARNING IN EARLY CHILDHOOD SETTINGS

In our introduction to this book, we described the challenge laid down to the chapter authors, to the following questions: *What is professional learning? Where does early childhood professional learning occur? What role are post developmental perspectives playing in current approaches to professional learning?* And, based on the authors' experience, research, and practice, *What are the challenges facing the early childhood field with respect to professional learning?* Each of the resulting chapters provides a window into the complexity of professional learning in early childhood settings and the potential of post-developmental perspectives to support teacher engagement with this complexity. In this final commentary, we reflect on the ideas, examples, and arguments the chapter authors have presented, and propose some potential directions for research and development in professional learning in ECE.

An initial analysis of the chapters in this book suggests that a post-developmental professional learning agenda in ECE is characterised by: 1) a reconsideration of the methodologies and methods for fostering professional learning used with, and by, practitioners; and 2) consideration of how practitioners and practitioner knowledge are situated within broader professional, academic, community, and political arenas with respect to the relationship between professional learning and children's developmental outcomes. We support this agenda and tentatively offer three questions we believe may be useful in framing future research in this area: First, what characterises the approaches to professional learning that are best suited to early childhood settings informed (or seeking to be informed), by post-developmental perspectives? and, second, What will be the impact of post-developmental perspectives as they change teacher thinking and action in early childhood education in these neo-liberal and postmodern times? As we reflect on these two questions, we simultaneously offer a third question, namely, what might be some potentially useful, and post-developmentally coherent, research directions for interrogating professional learning in ECE?

PROFESSIONAL LEARNING METHODOLOGIES AND METHODS

Each of the chapters in this book describes, either implicitly or explicitly, a preferred methodology and method of professional learning (as distinct from the research methodologies and methods adopted by the authors, which may or may

S. Edwards, J. Nuttall (eds.), Professional Learning in Early Childhood Settings, 131–137.

not mirror the methods encountered by the teachers). These include providing teachers with the opportunity to share narrative accounts of practice (e.g. the members of the Revolutionary Planning Group), direct instruction (e.g. educators qualifying for Early Years Professional Status), co-constructive relationships (Lisa and Sarah's experience of learning about sociocultural theory), and Developmental Work Research (Engeström, 2005) (the kindergarten teachers in the City of Casey). While these approaches differ with respect to method, we wonder whether there are some features underpinning these accounts that have the potential to move us toward a recognisable post-developmental methodology of professional learning.

First, and perhaps foremost, the chapters in this book are a characterised by a deep respect for the centrality of *experience* in teacher learning. By experience, we mean both the wisdom of practice accumulated in educational settings over time, and the ways in which this wisdom can itself be interrogated as part of developing practice. Jan Georgeson's account, in Chapter 8, of a professional learning and leadership model imposed through policy intervention, alerts us to the risks governments and communities take when they discount the accumulated wisdom of practitioners. This is not to romanticise or essentialise the experience accumulated by effective practitioners. Rather, we believe that effective approaches to professional learning in early childhood settings are characterised by a healthy respect for what practitioners and institutions already know and can do, and the subtlety with which good practice responds to distinctive places and times.

Second, we recognise that this hard-won professional expertise is not just a system of ideas, but a response to children, families, and contexts that is held *in the body* of practitioners, both individually and collectively. The implication of this is that effective approaches to professional learning in early childhood education recognise the emotional and visceral impacts that result from risk-taking, innovation, and change in a traditionally low-status, feminised profession that is also subject to intense scrutiny by clients and governments. All too often, professional 'development' in schools and early childhood settings is a euphemism for transmission (rather than interrogation) of ideas, and is designed to implement new policy directions, curriculum frameworks, or reductive models of 'what works'. We do not anticipate, nor do we advocate, a time when educators are not be held accountable for their practices but we would argue that approaches to professional learning that seek to govern the minds and actions of teachers are likely to be resisted. Mindy Blaise's description of the Revolutionary Planning Group (this volume) is one example of a site of resistance, and Alma Fleet and Catherine Patterson (Chapter 2) also mention, in passing, their experience of working in settings where teachers actively resisted externally-imposed 'Professional Development'.

These two claims – that professional learning is both experiential and embodied – imply methodologies that draw on phenomenological and hermeneutic principles to understand social phenomena. By attending to the 'lived experience' of teaching and learning, and to how meaning is constructed in particular places and times, researchers can both position early childhood educators as the 'experts' in their field, and capture something of this expertise to share with others. But we would argue that such approaches are insufficient to understand teacher learning in early childhood education in post-developmental times. The initial teacher education literature, for example, is replete with studies of teachers' 'perspectives', single-shot and small cohort studies, and studies which draw heavily on 'reflective practice' (Nuttall, Mitchell, & Seddon, 2006). These studies *describe* teacher learning in interesting ways but have only limited usefulness in identifying how best to *provoke* teacher learning. Post-developmental theories, such as sociocultural and cultural-historical activity theory, poststructuralism, and critical theory each attempt to make sense of the ways in which individual perspectives and social phenomena co-evolve and give meaning to the actions and activities comprising particular communities of practice (Beach, 1999). Methodologically, this moves the unit of analysis for research (and, by extension, professional learning) away from an exclusive psychological focus on the mind of individual teachers, to the complex interplay between personal, interpersonal, and collective forms of thinking and action. Furthermore, this allows researchers and professional developers to consider the role of teacher identity formation in relation to social context.

By bringing together these two claims (that teacher learning is individually and collectively experienced and individually and collectively embodied), we formulate a third claim: if teacher learning in early childhood settings depends on a synthesis of experience, identity, theory (formal and otherwise), and social action, then the best evidence of continuing professional learning will take the form of theories-in-action that are both pedagogically sound and context-specific. The New Zealand Ministry of Education has gone some way toward recognising and supporting this through its system of early childhood centre self-review (Ministry of Education, n.d.). This process depends on the identification of locally valued goals (albeit in concert with centrally developed expectations), context-specific forms of data, local analysis of this data by multiple stakeholders, and the de-privatisation of the experience of teachers, families, and children. When fully operational, such processes are both high-accountability and high-risk for early childhood educators, yet also hold out the promise of increased status and recognition of the complexity of educational work with young children, since these types of analyses emphasise what teachers do and how they too are learning. Significantly, the development of centres and programs is understood first at the collective level and not at the level of individual teachers.

A limitation inherent in phenomenologically-informed research approaches is the tendency to rely on self-report as a form of data generation. Self-report, and other forms of 'soft' data, such as narrative assessment of children's learning, leave researchers (and, by extension, the early childhood profession) open to accusations of 'insider' knowledge and lack of accountability, particularly with respect to children's learning. Philosophical and methodological rejoinders to these arguments have been thoroughly explored in the research literature (see, for example, Gage, 1989) but this remains a risky strategy in the present policy environment. In the United Kingdom, Australia, and New Zealand, where early childhood policy is dominated by neo-liberal discourses of human capital and the positioning of children as future contributors to the taxpayer base underpinning late-capitalist economies (Dahlberg & Moss, 2005; for a thoughtful analysis of this discussion in the Australian context, see Marcos, 2008). Robust alternatives are offered by professional learning and research approaches such as action research, Developmental Work Research (Engeström, 2005), professional learning circles, and institutional ethnography (Smith, 2005), which each offer specific strategies for interrogating the webs of social relationships characterising work sites. These approaches also have the potential to make explicit the relationship between policy, social relationships, organisational goals, and individual learning when the changes fostered by professional learning begin to be realised.

THE POTENTIAL OF POST-DEVELOPMENTAL PERSPECTIVES

Where governments are investing heavily in early childhood education with a view to minimising economic risk, there is the danger of assuming a direct, causal, and unidirectional relationship between professional learning, professional practice, children's experience, and children's learning outcomes, including future achievement at school; Wood (2004), for example, questions the impact of national curriculum initiatives in the UK and their impact on classroom practice in ECE. Practitioners and researchers alike know that the relationship between teacher learning and children's learning is far more complex and multivariate than politicians and bureaucrats would frequently like to believe. Furthermore, attempts to systematically model these relationships (e.g. between particular forms of initial teacher education, subsequent classroom practice, and children's achievement), both qualitatively and quantitatively, are only in their infancy. As Georgeson argues (this volume), conceptualising professional learning purely in cause and effect terms does not necessarily result in quality pedagogical experiences for children.

We argue that post-developmental approaches to professional learning in early childhood education aim to recognise the working practices, knowledges, theories, experiences and contexts of teachers as valid starting points for professional learning and engagement. In this way, the teachers in the Revolutionary Planning Group were able to imagine how they might adapt and transform their practice, and the teachers providing vignettes of their ethical dilemmas in Chapter 5 reveal their rich insight into practice as the starting point for their decision-making. To do otherwise means understanding teacher learning in ways that are at odds with the theoretical frameworks currently informing early childhood education, including cultural-historical theory, critical theory and poststructuralist perspectives. We argue, as do many of the authors in this book, that recognition of the complex relational work involved in being an early childhood teacher, rather than conceptualising teacher development solely as a linear, vertical phenomenon, is essential to fostering continued professional engagement and meaningful reflective practice.

Whilst readers of this volume will no doubt identify their own lines of inquiry, we believe a central issue in this area of research relates to how post-developmental perspectives will continue to influence the provision of early childhood education. In the introduction to this book we discussed how post-developmental perspectives are increasingly shifting the focus from traditional, normative, developmental conceptions of childhood to critical, cultural-historical, and other alternative approaches to understanding children, childhood, development and learning. These changes, which have all been influenced to a greater or lesser extent by the advent of postmodernism, necessitate new forms of professional learning. These new forms of adult development allow practitioners to engage with multiple ideas, theories, constructs, and practices in ways that challenge not only normative conceptions of development, but also the provision of transfer-oriented, 'one-stop' approaches to professional learning. This, in turn, suggests the need for research aimed at understanding what comprises effective professional learning from a post-developmental perspective. Furthermore, in addition to continuing the types of small-scale studies (collectively representing a tremendous resource about teacher learning) that are reported in this book, the early childhood field now has many opportunities to develop cross-national, comparative, multi-sectorial, and multi-method studies to give further empirical weight to research findings. These are strategies that capitalise upon the multiple entry points afforded by the diversity of the early childhood field, rather than viewing this diversity as a methodological problem or reinscribing long-standing hierarchies of legitimacy within the field (e.g. between kindergarten and infant programs, or between centre-based services and family day care). The early childhood field has experienced a rapid rise in profile in Australia, the United Kingdom, and New Zealand during the last two decades, which needs to be paralleled by growth in research into professional learning; otherwise, the knowledge and development of early childhood educators risks being positioned as a means to an end, rather than a legitimate end in itself, worthy of interrogation and celebration.

FINAL COMMENTS

This book began with modest intentions, seeking to examine approaches to professional learning in early childhood settings from post-developmental theoretical perspectives. In inviting contributions to this collection, we were interested to see how early childhood professional learning is being conceptualised in relation to changing cultural, social, economic, and technological times. The chapters suggest that practitioners, researchers, and teacher educators are grappling with, responding to, and, in some cases, resisting conceptual change. We see researchers as making important contributions to both describing and driving change in ECE. In order to do so, researchers will have to pay attention to multiple, simultaneous levels of change – from individual teachers through to national and transnational policy shifts – success stories as well as struggles, and to the consequences of professional learning for teacher identity, career progression, and the changing position of early childhood educators within wider discourses of education, parenting, and the participation of children in the economy and civil society. Such research will allow the early childhood field to not only make sense of how policy shapes early childhood education, but how the steadily increasing interest in post-developmental theories of teaching and learning, and the teachers who subscribe to these approaches, impact on the development of policy itself.

Furthermore, if researchers in early childhood education are to better understand the learning of children, families, students of early childhood teacher education, and, indeed, of early childhood academics themselves, there need to be more 'voices from the field' fore-grounded in discourses of continuing professional learning. There are many aspects of how adults learn in early childhood education that remain poorly understood, despite the willingness of practitioners to share their perspectives. One of these is the experience of learning across one's career in early childhood education, from undergraduate to graduate to experienced educator. A second potential research focus is the participation and learning of early childhood educators in multi-disciplinary and inter-professional early years settings, such as hospitals, children's hubs, and other integrated and co-located children's services. The complex relational work involved in being an early childhood educator is something that must be learned, yet it is one of the most difficult aspects of educational work to understand and to teach.

In this book, the term 'post-developmental perspectives' has been used as an umbrella for examining the many different theoretical and methodological approaches being employed by researchers and early childhood educators to examine the complexity of early childhood education and how this complexity both affords and constrains the practice of teaching. Ultimately though, the focus must return to the learning of educators, children, and families working together, moving beyond 'post-developmental professional learning' to examine how this particular theoretical and methodological movement can contribute to contemporary social practices in ways that celebrate the contribution of early childhood educators everywhere.

REFERENCES

Beach, K. (1999). Consequential transitions: A sociocultural expedition beyond transfer in education. *Review of Research in Education, 24*, 101–139.

Dahlberg, G., & Moss, P. (2005). *Ethics and politics in early childhood education.* New York: RoutledgeFalmer.

Engeström, Y. (2005). *Developmental work research: Expanding activity theory in practice.* Berlin: Lehmanns Media.

Gage, N. L. (1989). The paradigm wars and their aftermath: A "historical" sketch of research on teaching since 1989. *Educational Researcher, 18*(7), 4–10.

Marcos, A. (2008). *Australian early childhood policy and the education and care dichotomy.* Unpublished MEd thesis, Monash University, Melbourne.

Ministry of Education. (n.d.). *Self-review guidelines for early childhood education: Ngā aroahaeae whai hua.* Wellington, New Zealand. Retrieved October 20, 2008, from http://www.lead.ece. govt.nz/Publications/SelfReview/default.htm

Nuttall, J., Mitchell, J., & Seddon, T. (2006). Changing research contexts in teacher education in Australia: Charting new directions. *Asia-Pacific Journal of Teacher Education, 34*(3), 321–332.

Smith, D. E. (2005). *Institutional ethnography: A sociology for people*. Walnut Creek, CA: AltaMira Press.
Wood, E. (2004). A new paradigm war? The impact of national curriculum policies on early childhood teachers' thinking and classroom practice. *Teaching and Teacher Education, 20*(4), 361–374.

Joce Nuttall
Centre for Childhood Studies
Faculty of Education
Monash University
Susan Edwards
Centre for Childhood Studies
Faculty of Education
Monash University